"THE SCHOLAR AS PREACHER" SERIES

First edited by the Rev. JAMES HASTINGS, D.D.

---

38 George Street : T & T CLARK : Edinburgh, 2

NO UNCERTAIN SOUND

NO UNCERTAIN SOUND

BY

R. LEONARD SMALL, O.B.E., D.D.,
ST. CUTHBERT'S CHURCH, EDINBURGH

EDINBURGH : T. & T. CLARK, 38 GEORGE STREET
1963

© R. LEONARD SMALL 1963

PRINTED IN GREAT BRITAIN BY
MORRISON AND GIBB LIMITED
LONDON AND EDINBURGH
FOR
T. & T. CLARK, EDINBURGH

FIRST IMPRESSION 1963

CONTENTS

vii

CONTENTS

IV

THE NOTE OF URGENCY—WE MUST LOVE HIM TOO

I

MISSING NOTES IN CONTEMPORARY CHRISTIANITY

" My heart and my flesh crieth out for the living God."—
Ps. lxxxiv. 2.

O F all the sayings of Robert Burns one of the most
frequently quoted must surely be

" O wad some Power the giftie gie us,
To see oursels as ithers see us ! "

That is a prayer we all must echo often, especially on
those occasions when we step aside for a little to take
stock of our position and seek new strength for our
tasks. To see ourselves as others see us, to view the
setting of our normal life and work with the clarity
born of detachment, to bring to bear upon it a fresh
outlook—what a help that could be in restoring our
scale of values, and our sense of proportion. One
wonders sometimes how our modern, highly-organised
church-life, on either side of the Atlantic, would look
to some of the far-off founders of our faith.

If some of those who first fashioned this faith we
now possess could do " a Rip Van Winkle " and come
back from the sleep of ages, what would they think of
us to-day ? If the three famous Johns could return to
us—John Calvin, John Knox, and John Wesley—
what, do you imagine, would they think of us ? Surely
any of these most honoured guests would see much to
admire, and even envy. They would marvel at the
vast numbers who owe outward allegiance, at least,
to Christ through our several denominations, though
the exclusive spirit we sometimes show might rather
shock them. Well might we learn still from the great
words of Wesley : " Give me thine hand. I do not

say, ' Come thou over to my side ' nor ' Take me over
to thine '. But if thy heart be as my heart in the love
of Christ, give me thine hand." Knox, with his eager
interest in education, would admire our widespread,
carefully planned programmes of Christian education,
though, as he reviewed our " progress " since his own
time, he might dismiss some of our Graded Lessons as
milk and water stuff compared with the strong meat
of the Shorter Catechism ! Calvin, remembering his
Genevan system of a Church Order that held civic
power as well, would be intrigued by our tremendous
opportunities for influencing the whole community,
either individually, or through our corporate Christian
witness. What a pity he could not have been invited
to lead the prayers at the American Senate, or even at
the opening of the " Mother of Parliaments " ! John
the disciple would probably be struck most of all with
our buildings. Take him on a conducted tour of
church buildings, new and old, in London or even
Edinburgh, and how much he would see to admire.
For America one would like him to arrive by sea, and
record his first impressions of the fantastic New York
skyline. Would he think, one wonders, of the New
Jerusalem, or, perhaps, of Babylon ? It is a far cry
from the Upper Room at Jerusalem, the Room where
twelve men and their Master met so long ago, the
Room where the Risen Christ appeared to beaten men
behind closed doors, shut in with their fears—it is a
far cry from that to one of our great modern churches,
with its vast sanctuary, its halls and classrooms, its
office staff and specialised equipment, the almost
astronomical figures of its annual budget, its scores of
cars parked outside. One does wonder at times if a
person like John might not feel rather lost and start
looking round for the Master.

However that may be, one has the awkward feeling
that anyone who had known Christianity at the time
of any of these great leaders would miss something in
our contemporary Christianity, in spite of all its out-

ward strength and organization and efficiency. It is
not the kind of thing that is easy to define. You listen
to a concert pianist, and she gives a good performance,
competent and technically flawless, but it lacks—
something. You look at a modern painting, and it is
undeniably good, with both form and colour, but
again it lacks—something. In the same way there
are certain notes which have always been typical of a
Christian faith that is true and vital, and that one
misses in the life of almost all our churches to-day.
These are the notes that our imaginary visitors would
miss most if they came among us now.

They would miss first *the note of urgency*. " My
heart and my flesh crieth out for the living God ", says
the Psalmist, and one can hear the note of urgency
vibrating through the tones of his voice. That verse
calls to one's mind two pictures. One of our Scottish
country doctors, who spent a life-time serving the
scattered folk of a lonely area, tells in his reminiscences
how after a weary day he would be awakened out of
the sleep of sheer exhaustion by a persistent hammering
on the door, and when he stumbled to open it he would
find a desperate man, who had ridden miles over the
hills, and who cried : " Oh ! doctor, it's the wife.
You must come at once." As they went the doctor
noticed that the man's knuckles were broken and
bleeding with hammering on the door, so desperate
was the urgency of his need. The other is a scene
dramatically described by A. J. Cronin in his autobiography, *Adventures in Two Worlds*. He tells of a
mining district in Wales when he was a young doctor.
Some sixty men were entombed by a fall of rock, and
after days of bitter toil rescuers brought out thirty-
three men—dead. There was just an outside chance
that the rest had escaped into some old workings, and
for seven days, with a frenzy born of despair, men
toiled night and day to break through. They met
obstacle after obstacle, flood water, solid whinstone
rock, but at last the way was clear and they stumbled

forward through the old workings only to be brought up short by another fall of rock. In numbed silence they stood, utterly defeated, when suddenly they heard a strange persistent tapping, tap-tap, tap-tap, tap-tap-tap. It was the " jowling ", the signal a miner gives to let his mate know he is working in the same seam. It could only have come from men still alive on the other side of that rock barrier. Like a flash the rescuers got to work again, one after the other, tearing through the living rock, with a hopeful urgency now, and they did break through, and they brought out every man alive.

Now, where is there in our contemporary Christianity any suggestion of that spirit of desperate need, that feeling that here is a matter of life and death, that not a moment is to be lost ? Is not our religion a rather quiet and respectable affair, unhurried and unflurried, its ways of worship familiar to the point of boredom to many of our people ? Would any of these imaginary visitors, dropping in unannounced at your church or mine, get the impression that here is the most vital and urgent issue in the lives of the worshippers, that nothing counts so much as what is happening here on Sunday ? We have lost the note of urgency from the pew.

Is it, partly, because we have lost it in the pulpit ? An old man, a deep thinker, said to his minister : " You know, when I was a boy the preacher nearly every Sunday took you up by the scruff of the neck and held you out over the pit of hell, until the smell of the fire and brimstone got into your lungs and fair choked you. It may have been all wrong, but at least it made you feel ' I've got to hurry up and do something to keep out of this '. Nowadays you preachers don't believe in hell, any more. Maybe you're right, but you haven't put anything in its place, and you give the people the impression that there isn't any hurry about anything." Is it going to take the smell of a nuclear cataclysm and the fear of radioactive fall-out to give us back the sense of urgency, the stark realisation that there is not much time left ?

Have we, the preachers of this atomic age, forgotten that the gospel we preach is joined to the most urgent issues anywhere in human life ?   There is nothing so important for any man as that he should get right with God, that he should find the full, rich life which Christ alone offers, that he should enter into that new relationship which lasts through time into eternity. You may call it being born again, or being converted, or finding Christ, or accepting Christ, the final meaning is the same—here is a matter of life and death, more literally than any other we ever face.   When we preach let us remember the privilege and responsibility of our task.   The greatest service any human being can perform for any other is to help that other to be right with God.   It is our task and our duty—uniquely so in most communities, to perform that service.   Let us discharge that duty with the same controlled sense of urgency as the doctor shows when his skill and experience bring a child, alive and unhurt, into this world ;   as the brain surgeon displays when his careful fingers handle the delicate material which is the stuff of life itself.

One Christmas Day, many years ago, a Scandinavian cargo ship was driven by a north-easterly gale on the rocks near the mouth of the Firth of Forth.   She was swept constantly by heavy seas and was in danger of breaking up.   The only way to save her crew was by rocket apparatus, and two boxes of carefully coiled light line were carried down to the nearest point on the rocks.   The coastguard set up his rocket-tripod, made fast the line to the tail and fired the rocket.   Away it soared, straight for the doomed ship, and then the gale caught it and swept it away like a child's paper streamer, to fall uselessly in the sea.   There was only one more box of line, the last hope of safety for these men.   You can imagine with what desperate care the line was attached and the rocket set.   This time it was aimed, not straight at the ship, but up-wind, away from the wreck. Three times the coastguard held the match ready, and each time a stronger gust dissuaded him. Then he lit the rocket and it soared out far past the stern, nowhere near the target. Then the gale took charge, and blew it right across the ship, abaft the funnel. The watching men dashed out and caught the light line, pulling it in. To it was attached a heavier rope and to that one still heavier, as thick as your wrist. On this was a board with instructions in eight different languages, telling the men where and how to make it fast. The other end was anchored fast to the rocks and over that rope-bridge in a breeches-buoy, the crew were hauled, one by one, to safety.

Here, surely, is a parable for us preachers. We must have the same urgent desire for the " saving " of men, the same serious sense that our word may be their last chance. We must take account of the changing winds of thought and current opinion, and use them to carry and not deflect our message. We must persuade men, in whatever language they understand, to lay hold upon the hope of salvation we offer them in Christ's name, and, once they have done their part, we may not rest till we have brought them, saved and safe, to His feet. God give us back the note of urgency.

The second missing note is *the note of joy*. Moffatt's translation of this verse from Ps. lxxxiv. runs as follows : " Now soul and body thrill with joy for the living God ". There cannot be the least doubt that a rare kind of joy has been the hall-mark of vital Christianity in every generation. It was said of the first-century Christians that they were " absurdly happy, and always getting into trouble ". When one of the Covenanting preachers, a mere lad, was put to death for his faith in the Grassmarket of Edinburgh, he mounted the steps to the scaffold with a glow of joy on his face. " Every step", he cried, " is a step nearer Christ." In our own century Sir Wilfred Grenfell of Labrador wrote to a Canadian nursing sister in hospital : " Come and spend your vacation in our Mission Hospital. You won't get any pay, and you'll have to pay your own travelling expenses, but I promise you that you will be happier than you ever were in your life." She accepted the challenge and after her vacation had ended she wrote him saying : " You were right. I have never known such deep joy and real happiness. Can I come back to stay ? " Yes, there is a rare kind of joy which Jesus described as His own peculiar gift to His followers.

Do we have it to-day ? Look in imagination on the faces of the congregation you see Sunday by Sunday. Do they suggest to you radiant joy ? What is wrong ? Too many of us are far too negative in our religion, it does no more for us than set before us a series of ideals too high for us to attain, and remind us of all the things we ought not to do. No wonder it was said of a character in an English novel of a generation ago : " Mrs. Bindle was only religious enough to be miserable ". Someone may at once object, asking how any thinking person can be expected to be cheerful in days like these, what with the threat of nuclear warfare leading to total destruction, the menace of Communism, the growth of materialism, the rising cost of living, and all our other woes and worries. But Christianity never was a simple faith for easy days, it belongs in this kind of setting. Many children, on both sides of the Atlantic, have been delighted with the plantation stories of Uncle Remus, with their wonderful animal characters, and their deep human wisdom. There is one particularly memorable scene when Brer Rabbit, after hosts of narrow escapes, was caught at last by his arch-enemy, Brer Fox. While the captor was debating how best to finish off this bane of his existence, Brer Rabbit began at once to plead that whatever cruel fate might be his he should not be thrown into the brier-patch. He pled so earnestly and so piteously that, of course, Brer Fox decided what would be the one most fitting fate, and, taking the rabbit by the

hind legs, hurled him into the heart of the brier-patch.
There was a little silence, and then from the midst of
the briers an irrepressible voice called out : " Bred
an' bawn in a brier-patch, Brer Fox, bred an' bawn
in a brier-patch ! " Christianity was bred and born in
a brier-patch ; it began with a homeless child and a
family of D.P.'s, and it led up to the public execution
of an insignificant provincial, done to death by a great
militaristic power. It is quite at home in this kind of
setting.

There is much in our situation to make us gloomy,
but is there nothing to make a Christian joyful ?
When Oliver Cromwell lay a-dying his friends gathered
round his bed with long faces, and the women started
weeping. The old warrior raised himself on his elbow
and growled out : " Is there nobody here will praise
God ? " What a challenge, to us all. Too often we
who are preachers have been guilty of that worst of
" Spoonerisms "—we have made more of the " tearful
chidings " than of the " cheerful tidings " of the gospel.
Have we forgotten that we have a gospel for days like
these—good news, glad tidings of great joy ? A
generation notoriously in search of a thrill but really
looking for true happiness seldom thinks of looking to
us who *are* the Church, for we do not appear ourselves
to have found the secret of joy. God give us back the
note of joy.

The final missing note is *the note of triumph*. The
operative word of our text in this connection is the
word " living "—" my heart and my flesh crieth out
for the *living* God ". Too many of us, deep down,
have ceased really and truly to believe in the victorious
power of the living God. We really believe in a God
who did great things, unmistakably, in the past, but
does them no longer. This is the real reason why so
many Christians, both in the pulpit and the pew, are
so pathetically defeatist. We believe men like D. H.
Lawrence, when he wrote to Katherine Mansfield :
" Don't worry, Kate. Jesus is a back-number ", or

the doctor in Tennyson's poem when he declares to the nurse in " In the Children's Hospital " that " the good Lord Jesus has had his day ". We feel in our bones that the human situation has got out of hand, even God's hand. We see humanity sliding deeper and deeper into the abyss of self-destruction. We lose heart at our own job, for what is the good of life and service if " there's no future in it " ? And all about us men and women are wistfully looking for conviction and certainty, eager for the note of triumph and victory. Do we really imagine that the Lord's arm is shortened, that He has had a stroke, and cannot save any more ? Do we honestly believe that Communism or materialism, or any other " ism " of our time, is too strong or too subtle for God ? Do we not realise that God has put too much of Himself into this troubled, sinning, bewildered world ever to desert it now ?

A Christian these days may often be defeated, but he has no sort of right to be defeatist. In the life of George Macdonald, the novelist, we are told how, when he was a sickly student, his mother took him to the mountains of Switzerland. One day they were visiting a neighbouring village, the sickly lad and his frail little mother. As they walked through the village street a great darkness covered the sky and a rain-cloud broke. The two ran into the village church for shelter. Hardly had they entered when an earthquake shook the mountain, and the ground quivered as the hide of a horse might quiver under the sting of a gnat. Then there was a slight lull, and when the roar of the earthquake returned it was mingled with a strange, new sound from the organ of that little church, the great opening chords of the *Hallelujah Chorus*. That was the frail woman's answer to an earthquake : " Hallelujah ! for the Lord God omnipotent reigneth." Is there any better answer to the doubts and fears, the real and legitimate forebodings we have for the future ? This is no day for lilting trivialities, or for mournful numbers in the minor key. Let not our imaginary visitors nor our real and actual people miss the trumpet-note of triumph.

> " The kingdoms of the earth go by
> In purple and in gold ;
> They rise, they flourish, and they die,
> And all their tale is told.
> One Kingdom only is divine,
> One banner triumphs still,
> Its King . . . a servant,
> And its sign ? . . . a gibbet on a hill."

Our God is marching on. God in Christ " hath sounded forth the trumpet that shall never call retreat ".

THE NOTE OF TRIUMPH—
FAITH FACES THE CHALLENGE
OF SUFFERING

1

SUFFERING AS A TEST

" The Lord gave, and the Lord hath taken away ; blessed be the name of the Lord."—Job i. 21.

FROM the earliest beginnings of conscious human life men have concerned themselves with the problem of suffering. They have observed the fact of suffering, for they could not evade it, and in trying to deal with it they have often turned to whatever gods there be. So primitive man took what measures he deemed desirable to propitiate the spirits that inhabited stone and wood, and rock and tree, so that the first crops he learned to cultivate might not be blighted and withered, that his toil might not be wiped out by flood, that his children should not die from some mysterious pestilence, nor his enemies work his ruin. Primitive peoples to this day still do the same. The Jew made the problem more difficult. He declared that life was not just at the mercy of capricious and quite unpredictable powers, it was controlled by a righteous God, who demanded of men that they should do justly, and love mercy, and walk humbly with their God. The Jew had a deep sense of the sovereignty of God over all things, he asserted His control alike over Nature and human history, and the theme song of his philosophy of life was " The Lord sitteth King over the flood ". By so doing he made the problem of suffering much more acute, for how are men to walk humbly and unquestioningly with an all-controlling God who, on palpable evidence which none of us can evade, appears so often to do far from justly, and acts not only without mercy but with a kind of calculated cruelty that simply staggers our faith ?

The Book of Job is a great and honest and sincere attempt to face the problem thus made acute, rejecting those easy, cheap solutions which are such a mockery of real suffering and agonising doubt. Its message is couched in dramatic form and is written with a beauty of language which must always merit our study. More important still it faces bravely a problem that is always with us, and that is ever new. Each year brings its tragic succession of disasters, storms, floods and avalanches, the horror of a mine disaster in Germany, where almost three hundred lives were lost, the tragic death roll of the crash of an air liner near New York with the loss of all on board ; hardly a week passes without some News Bulletin laying this problem of suffering heavily on our minds and hearts. Most ministers have had the experience of visiting on the same day a hospital ward where some thirty children lie crippled in diverse ways, and, in direct contrast, a geriatric hospital full of old people. The sight of these old folk, sitting staring empty-eyed, as if the light of life had already gone out and they were only waiting the release of death, and the children, suffering such terrible handicaps, albeit so cheerfully for the most part, makes us wonder with a deep sense of perplexity why we, who are taught to regard ourselves as the children of a loving God, should be called upon, all the way from childhood to old age, to suffer so in body, mind and spirit. Perhaps a careful study of the message of this Book of Job may point the way to some kind of answer.

The Prologue to the Book sets the scene and introduces the first main constructive idea. Let us sketch the setting again. Here is a good man, a man whose quality of goodness is described both negatively and positively, " perfect and upright, one that feareth God, and escheweth evil ". God has prospered him alike in possessions and family, for he has seven sons and three daughters. They seem to be a happy, harmonious family, for they meet regularly in turn in the home of each of the seven brothers. Job is careful to sanctify them, for at the end of each week's round of visits he carries out sacrifices of purification lest any of them should have " sinned in their hearts ". In other words, he is at great pains to do all that God might require of him. It is established, therefore, from the first, that our study concerns a good and innocent man, and so we are carried right away into the very heart of the problem of suffering. There is no problem in the suffering of a bad man. If a man plays fast and loose with the laws of health, physical, mental, moral or spiritual, if he abuses himself and suffers for it, if his body degenerates, his mind deteriorates, his spiritual faculties become atrophied, that is no problem ; the only problem is that such a man may seem to get away with it for so long. But this is the cruel problem of the suffering of the innocent.

Now the scene changes. As in some modern plays use is made of a revolving stage, so the author of this drama employs a stage on two levels ; we are now transported to a higher level, to the Courts of Heaven, where the Sons of God are met in council, and with them Satan. In this Book " Satan " is really a title— " the Adversary ". His function might be roughly compared to that of a Procurator-Fiscal in Scotland, for his duty is to detect the sons of men in any kind of misdemeanour or crime and arraign them before God. The Lord asks Satan if he has observed the goodness of Job. It is thus made plain that God is aware of the uprightness of His servant, that He delights in it, and is proud of it. What a grand thought, that any of us blind and blundering mortals should be able so to live that God should be proud of us ! It is as if the Lord challenged Satan with Job ;

" Even you, with your nose for smelling out evil, can you find anything wrong in Job ? " But the Adversary has been rendered deeply cynical by his long experience of seeking out the worst in human nature, and suggests that Job is good only because goodness so unmistakably pays. Here again is an incidental and implied challenge to us all. Why are we good, in so far as we manage to be good ? Out of love and respect for God, from a desire to do that which is well-pleasing in His sight, or because it pays ? Satan quite boldly suggests that if it is made plain to Job that goodness does not pay he will soon turn and curse God. Taking up the challenge God makes of Job a test case. He is testing not only Job's personal reaction to this trial but the responsiveness of human nature. Has God in fact succeeded in creating persons capable of such fellowship with God, such sharing of His mind and heart and will that, though terribly tried they will still do what He desires ? Anyhow the test is accepted, the permission is given, but God's ultimate control is maintained, limits are set to Satan's power ; he is not granted absolute freedom, for he must not lay his hand on Job himself.

Then the scene changes again to the level of earth, and we are called upon to witness a succession of disasters. Blow after blow falls on Job, and every detail of the description is significant. The sons and daughters are eating and drinking " in their eldest brother's house ". That is to say, the round of visits has just begun, the process of sanctification has just been carried out, they are safe now, if ever they can be. We are shown a quiet, peaceful, pastoral scene, the oxen ploughing and the asses feeding beside them. Suddenly the raiders come sweeping in from the desert; it is soon over and they are off again carrying their spoil, and leaving a trail of death behind them. Let that one scene stand for all that men have suffered from the violence of the enemy. Let the cries of the dying there give voice to all the cries of the centuries, proclaiming man's inhumanity to man. Let the Sabeans represent raiders of every colour and sort ; they are as old as the cave man, and as modern as the Congo or Algiers. Whether they come sweeping out of the glare of the desert or droning out of the darkened skies they leave behind, when they have passed, the same smouldering ruins and empty roof-trees, the same twisted bodies, the same staring eyes, pointing their mute question to an unheeding Heaven, the same cry of those left alive who would be better dead. There is no need to expatiate, for we have all seen too much and know the situation only too well. Next comes a natural disaster, for fire from heaven burns up the sheep. What a horror it is to see the dead animals, trapped by fire, or swept away by flood, a man's toil of the years, all he has built up swept away in a night, his plans shattered and in ruins. One pictures the flooded acres which in so many lands have spoiled the farmer's work, drowned his livestock and invaded his home, or the dead lambs bestrewing our Scottish hillsides when a bitter Spring has left them no chance of survival. What callous, cruel loss at the hands of " Mother Nature " ! But Job is not yet utterly destitute, he still has his camels, true wealth in that kind of society ; he can move away to fresh pasture and a safer place. He can still provide for his family with what is left. Yet another messenger of doom arrives, telling of yet another raid, and declaring that the last of his outward possessions is gone. But he still has his family, and a family are in the end the best investment, they constitute a man's true wealth. With his seven stalwart sons and three fine daughters he can still start again. All is not lost as long as they have each other. Then comes the news that the family, too, are lost, all of them in one all-embracing disaster, they are utterly wiped out, not one left. Perhaps a modern parallel will help us to realise the sheer tragedy of Job's loss. One day in 1941 I was asked by a Commanding Officer to say what I could to one of his men, who sat in a small room by himself waiting for the train to take him from his station in Scotland to his " home " in Liverpool. That man had just received the news that in an enemy raid the night before his home had sustained a direct hit. In it at the time were his wife and three children, and his own parents who had gone to keep the wife company. All that he possessed, his furniture, his goods and chattels, were dust and rubble, and all six of the people he loved were dead. He just sat there, staring into emptiness, everything gone. Such was the situation of Job. What we are studying is the story of a man who has suffered terribly, who has lost everything, and has every right to curse God.

Such then is the setting of the stage for our drama, and there are two main points which we must observe and record at the outset.

This Book teaches throughout that the suffering it describes is sent, or at least permitted by God. Satan, the Adversary, actually inflicts the suffering and disaster but he does it only with God's knowledge and consent. There is a very important principle here, which demands most careful thinking. All the characters in the drama clearly regard the suffering as being sent by God. Job's friends assume that it has been sent as a judgment on or punishment for some secret sin. This Job indignantly and persistently denies, yet he himself still assumes that it is sent, that God is behind it all, that He is responsible. Now a very little thought will show us that there is a great deal of suffering which God does not send, and for which He is not responsible. When some woman, turned monster in human form, herds her fellow-women into the gas chamber at Dachau, is that an act of God ? When a father and mother—save the name—take it in turn to beat a child of three until she dies, is that an act of God ? A gay and laughing young girl, without a care in the world, went into hospital for a very trivial, minor operation, was given the wrong anaesthetic and died under it. Was that an act of God ? No ! It was an act of criminal human negligence. Even when we are trying to understand natural disasters we must not think of God giving instructions to the powers of His universe to strike. We dare not think of Him summoning some monster of hidden turbulence, long and safely chained beneath the crust of the tiny island of Tristan da Cunha and bidding it " Go, drive these presumptuous human beings from this little corner of My wide domains. They are becoming too settled, and taking too much for granted ". Neither can we imagine Him allocating to a particularly violent hurricane the task of sweeping up the Florida coast, to smash the luxury homes which are the expression of the power of the " almighty " dollar. We just cannot picture the God and Father of our Lord, Jesus Christ, " sending " His winds and waves, His floods and avalanches about their duties of destruction. And yet, and yet, God is still responsible ; for if this is still God's world, and He is still in control, none of these things could happen except with His knowledge and consent. God is still responsible for the evil, the terrible evil He has left us free to do to each other, and for the terrifying powers of this strange world in which He has set us to live.

This is very important. At first sight it seems to make the problem even worse. But try to consider the matter from the point of view of those who actually suffer, or endure the agony of watching their loved ones suffer, those, for example, who have to receive home the charred remains of loved ones lost in the New York air disaster. Does it really help them if you suggest that there is in life some evil power, fighting against God and often winning real victories, a power of evil that now and then gets out of hand and runs amuck, and that this is the explanation of the suffering they have to face ? Is it not better, whatever it costs, to keep the picture of God in control, setting limits to the power of evil, making it serve His purpose, letting it happen—yes—but still not losing grip ? Ask those who have really suffered and they will tell you that you can go on bearing it, trusting where you cannot understand, if you believe, in this deep and sustaining sense, that God sent it, that it comes with His knowledge and consent, and therefore with His power and wisdom and love still at work in it.

The other truth that should be noted and recorded is that the purpose of the suffering is to test Job. This is a good place to start our thinking on this difficult problem, for here is something suffering actually does in our own clear experience, and this thought at least links suffering to a purpose that is both positive and worthwhile. Beyond all question suffering does test us all when it comes. It is a fact of observation and experience that suffering of the same quantity and quality may come to different people and they will all react differently according to the kind of people they are. Some are, unquestionably, refined and strengthened by what they have to suffer ; they find new depths in themselves ; out of their own suffering they distil, by some mysterious alchemy, a new sympathy and a larger compassion for the sorrows of others. There are also those who simply crumple up under suffering, rail at God and fate, cannot see why God should have done this to them. They turn to self-pity, take a delight in feeling sorry for themselves, and love to tell of their misfortunes. Nothing so tests us, reveals what we are, as suffering. It may well be that we are moved to ask : " Why should God thus put us to the test ? " It all depends what we think life is for. If the horizons of our thinking are bounded by this human existence, here and now ; if our chief end, and God's, is to enjoy the maximum of comfort and pleasure ; if the ideal for life is that a good time should be had by all, then, of course, such testing can serve no good purpose. But if this present life is intended as a preparation and apprenticeship for another and fuller kind of life ;

if it is designed to provide opportunities to prove and develop depth of character and fineness of personality, to reveal the grandeur of humanity at its best, then such testing has a clear and discernible purpose.

The final and abiding impression we carry away from our study of the Prologue to the Book of Job is that of the tremendous trust God reposes in His much-tried servant. One of the worst sufferers I have ever known was a particularly frail little woman, constantly wracked with pain. She had lost count of the number of operations she had undergone, and had suffered every kind of personal disaster, but she still resolutely refused merely negatively to accept her suffering. One day, out of her more than ample time to think and to think deeply about her personal situation, she said : " You know, I feel that this suffering is something with which God is trusting me." What a great thought, that the degree of suffering God sends, or allows to come with His knowledge and consent, is the measure of His tremendous trust in us ! If He should ever so terribly trust any of us, may He give us grace to rise to the dignity of Job's grand response : " the Lord gave, and the Lord hath taken away ; blessed be the name of the Lord ".

2

THE PAIN THAT IS HARDEST TO BEAR

" After this opened Job his mouth, and cursed his day."—
Job iii. 1.

WE have seen from the dramatic and moving first
chapter of this Book that the writer is pre-
senting the experience of an innocent man, who has
suffered blow after blow, and has every reason to be
bitter. We have learned that, however much it may
seem to deepen the mystery, it is in the end helpful
to remember that both for natural disasters and for
the evil men do to each other God is ultimately responsible, since none of them could come without His
knowledge and consent. We have learned, therefore,
to think of suffering as being, in this sense, " sent ",
related somehow to a constructive purpose, and we
have laid hold of the belief that, as in the Prologue,
the Council of Heaven made plain the purpose, so
there is a realm of being where the meaning of suffering
will one day be made plain. It is good to believe
amid all the mystery of suffering that the words of
the old Hymn are true

" I'll bless the hand that guided,
I'll bless the heart that planned,
When throned where glory dwelleth
In Immanuel's land."

We have further noted, as a fact of experience, that
suffering does test us all when it comes, revealing in
some the hidden flaws in faith or character, discovering
in others unsuspected strength. We have watched
with growing admiration how nobly Job rises to the
occasion, how splendidly and with what dignity he
stands the test.

The writer might have left it at that, and still put us in his debt. But the story is only beginning, the plot thickens, we are carried even deeper into the mystery of suffering. The matter, apparently, cannot be allowed to rest there, and the scene changes again from this vale of tears to the Courts of Heaven. With considerable dramatic effect the previous description of the Council of the Sons of God is repeated, word for word until the point where the Lord says of Job : " and still he holdeth fast his integrity, although thou movedst me against him, to destroy him without cause ". One can almost hear the note of pride and triumph in the voice of the Lord whose trust in His servant has been so splendidly vindicated. How daring the touch which is added in the last phrase, almost as if the Almighty regretted having agreed to the test, as it were, against His better judgment ! But the Adversary is not yet finished. He proceeds to argue that the test has been insufficient. Job has not yet been touched on the right spot, all the hurt is outside himself, he has lost only his possessions and his children. How unbelievably cynical, to suggest that the loss of his entire family has never touched the man himself ! And Satan makes this suggestion to the God concerning whom only a few pages further on in our Bible this stands written : " Like as a father pitieth his children, so the Lord pitieth them that fear him ". Anyhow, a further test is suggested and agreed upon. The guard is lifted still further so that Job's own person is now open to attack, but even now Satan is not given complete liberty, God is still holding the reins, and Job's life itself may not be endangered. With devilish ingenuity the Adversary carries out this fresh attack. He " smote Job ", we read, " with sore boils from the sole of his foot unto his crown. And he took him a potsherd to scrape himself withal ; and he sat down among the ashes ". Job himself in some of his speeches describes his own symptoms in fuller and often horrible detail and the experts are agreed that what he is describing is a particularly horrible form of leprosy. The account given makes it quite plain that this dread disease had not infected one limb or part of his body alone, his infection was total and complete. In this hopeless condition—for remember leprosy was a disease for which there was no known treatment of alleviation, much less cure—his wife pleads with him to curse God and be done with it, far better dead than living such a life. His friends come and offer their silent sympathy, sitting beside him without uttering a word for seven whole days and nights. Then, at last, Job breaks down utterly. Why ? We must study this question very carefully, for it is supremely important that we should strive to understand what is the sort of suffering that is hardest to bear, that can break down a brave man's resistance, and bring him to the point beyond which faith cannot go on, but must yield to doubt and despair. What kind of suffering is it that can make a man not only wish he were dead but curse the day he was born ?

Any attempt to understand Job's feelings must remind us that there are kinds and degrees of the pain a man may personally suffer. We may well pause to underline that word " personally ", for there is truth in Satan's cynicism, and there is a real sense in which it is only that which hurts a man's own skin that truly comes home to him. A physiologist, a neurologist and a psychologist may go the rounds of the wards, making meticulous notes of different types of pain, and of the varying human reactions to each. But let any one of these three " experts " suddenly fall a prey to a perforated gastric ulcer, and the agony gripping his vitals becomes something quite different from what he previously knew of pain. That reminds us of a fact we must continually keep in view throughout this enquiry. We are not really looking for a neat theory of suffering that will cover all the facts adduced, with all the data neatly pigeon-holed. We are searching for a means of dealing with pain and suffering

when they come to us and ours.   In the average congregation there will be, one hopes, at least a proportion
of young people.   To them, all this talk about the
problem of suffering may seem, at the moment, quite
academic and abstract, outwith their experience.
They would do well to remember that nothing is
more certain than this—at some time, sooner or later,
they, too, will be forced to face up to this problem,
and there is nothing so pathetic as the sight of someone, still young and of limited experience, suddenly
confronted with the fact of suffering and with no idea
how to think of or to handle such a problem.   There
is real point in the story of the dying Scot, who, being
asked by his daughter if she should read the Scripture
to him, replied : " No need, lassie.   I ha'e theekit
[thatched] my hoose in the calm weather ".   May
these studies help some at least of our young folk to
have the house of their faith well thatched when the
storm of suffering comes whirling about it.   Suffering
is always a problem for faith, but the greatest problem
is not merely how to think straight about it but how
to handle it victoriously.

   It is most revealing to try to understand what were
the elements in the pain that broke down Job's resistance.   Much of it, obviously, was physical.   The whole
body was affected with horrible eruptions, and a
dreadful wasting away of the flesh.   In itself no single
part was unbearably painful, not like the pain, for
example, of a stone in the kidney, the pain of which
the patient may say : " It had me climbing the walls ".
There is pain of a kind that comes in waves of agony,
which can reach the point at which the system can
stand no more, and when, as in an amputation before
the days of anaesthetics, the patient mercifully faints
from pain.   This pain was not like that, it just went
on all the time.   What is more, it was pain that had no
meaning, and that is a vital point.   Some pain has
meaning.   Pain can provide a warning in time before
irreparable damage is done ; pain can guide the

surgeon's probe, or the healing knife to the focal point of danger. Anyone who has undergone a major operation understands the distinction here. Before the operation you are in pain, so bad, perhaps, that you would undergo any risk rather than submit to it any more. After the operation you may still be in pain, even severe pain, but this is different, this is the pain of healing up, and you can bear it, for it has meaning. Job's pain had no meaning ; it was the kind about which nothing can be done.

But the purely physical was the least of it. There was a worse element of mental and spiritual anguish. Think of Job sitting among the ashes, a picture of most utter degradation. A little later in the Book he cries out : " I am become loathsome to myself ". All through the Bible one can sense the horror of leprosy. To be a leper was the most dreadful and degrading of fates. To be a leper was to know oneself beyond hope, incurable, doomed for ever to a life of ostracism and uselessness. The man who was so careful about the sanctifying of his family was bound to be fastidious about himself. And now he has come to this ! Add that element of mental and spiritual anguish, and pain becomes far worse to bear. In the summer of 1944, some weeks after D Day, some branches of the Woman's Guild in Edinburgh adopted each a Ward in the Royal Infirmary to supply with afternoon teas and home-baking the wounded men brought back from Normandy. In one of these wards was a sergeant whom his weekly visitor came to know unusually well. He had been badly smashed by a land-mine and eventually had to have his leg off above the knee. One particular day the visitor found him looking very white and drawn and obviously in a bad state of mind and nerves. " It's getting this stump dressed," he said. " Sister is very good about it, but it hurts like hell, and I dread the next time. I'm afraid I cry out like a coward before all these other men." He was adding mental agony, the thought of disgracing his manhood, to his physical pain. Or here is a young lad in his twenties, one of the remaining victims of tuberculosis. He insists on regarding himself as being somehow unclean, will never shake your hand, will hardly allow you to enter his room, for fear you be contaminated by the terrible thing he has become. He gives himself no sort of chance by adding to his already heavy physical burden this weight of mental anguish. Or here is a mother bravely " tholing " her pain—and how much better most women are at " tholing " than most men ! —but all the while tormenting herself with worry, as to what will happen to the family if she does not get better soon, or, perhaps ever. Add to physical suffering all the pain of being a man, of being vulnerable in mind and spirit too. That kind of suffering seems hardest to bear.

Two further thoughts come to us at this point in the drama of Job. A new character here appears on the stage, the wife of Job. Much cheap scorn has been poured upon her head, as if she were just the final irritation, making full the cup of her husband's misery. Surely we must think a little more deeply than that. If she was his wife, she was also, presumably, the mother of his children. Those seven stalwart sons and three fine daughters were hers as much as Job's, and she has lost them all. She has suffered, too, suffered, indeed, as only a mother can suffer from the loss of the children to whom she has given life. Part of her very self has been taken away. If you heard of a mother who lost four sons in the war you would bow your head in hushed reverence for her sorrow. This woman has lost all ten children at one fell swoop, and she has suffered terribly. Do you not think she suffers further when she sees her husband in his truly pathetic condition ? The point about her part in the drama, appearing as she does for a moment, speaking one bitter line, and then making her exit, is that she cracks before Job does. She cries to him to end it all, to curse God and die. She cannot stand any more to see him like that.

Surely his words : " Thou speakest as one of the
foolish women speaketh. What ? shall we receive
good at the hand of God, and shall we not receive
evil ? ", are not meant as a rude rebuke, but rather a
reproof touched with gentleness. He still says " we ",
as if to suggest that they two have shared the receiving
of joy, and now also the suffering of evil. That is what
hurts her most, for here is something that simply
cannot be shared. It hurts most of all to watch someone
you love suffering, and not be able to share it, to take
the suffering, or at least some of it upon yourself.
Here is a mother staggering into the Surgical Out-
Patient Department, wild-eyed, hugging to her breast
her terribly-burned child. You know at once that it
would hurt her far less if she could take the shock of
those awful burns into her own body. Here is a strong
man, fitness personified, sitting in one of the wards by
the screened bed where his wife lies, helpless in her
abysmal weakness. He has given her two blood
transfusions already and they will not let him give any
more. There is nothing he can do to take her weakness
into his strength, and therein lies his agony. No, it is
no accident that the wife of Job came sooner than he
did to the breaking-point. Suffering is often a bigger
problem for those who watch ; that is the pain that is
hardest to bear.

It is also true that the suffering that cannot be
understood is hard to bear. It is now that we note
the entry of the three friends, so notorious as Job's
comforters. In actual fact they seem tactfulness
itself. They agree to go together and so avoid that
repetition of sorrow which too often imposes strain on
a sufferer. They fail at first to recognise him, so
changed is he. They weep in real and sincere sympathy ;
they sit beside him in the dust. They do all that men
can to put themselves in his place. They keep silence
for seven days, realising that words are useless. It is
this well-meaning sympathy that finally breaks him
down. For how could they ever understand ? They

can never really put themselves in his place. The arguments they proceed to develop make this only too plain. No one can understand unless he has been through it himself, no one can meet him there in the depth of his misery, no one can give him real sympathy, no one—not even, nay, least of all, God. If He did, He would not allow it. So we find ourselves, inevitably and irresistibly, driven by the stark needs of this intolerable situation to take a leap beyond Job. We find ourselves looking, not down in futile pity on Job as he sits among the ashes, but up in utter humility at another Sufferer. We find ourselves remembering that the word we use for the worst kind of pain is " excruciating " agony, and that at the heart of that adjective is the word " crux ", " crucis ", meaning " a cross ". On that Cross we picture hours of dull, ignoble pain, complete desolation and utter degradation, the mind darkened by doubt, the spirit assailed by a sense of desertion and total failure. Looking, we know we are watching something Job could never know, God taking upon Himself the pain that is hardest to bear, seeing it from the inside, truly understanding.

THEORIES THAT ARE MOCKED BY FACT

" How forcible are right words ! but what doth your arguing reprove ? "—Job vi. 25.

THERE is something rather terrible and almost literally " shocking " about the spectacle of a good and fine and brave man utterly broken down. It is quite tragic to see Job after all he has been through and all he has stood so nobly, utterly collapsed and crying out that he wishes he had never been born. His cry is not less pathetic because it is couched in beautiful and lyrical language any more than Milton's cry about the bitter burden of his blindness is less pathetic because he makes it into a sonnet, or any more than David's lament over his son Absalom is less pathetic because it is a lyrical outburst of sorrow. It is deeply tragic to see Job thus broken down, and it is probably because his three friends feel this that they are impelled to say something. They just cannot stand the strain of keeping silent any longer. The three of them, who are traditionally supposed to represent different ages and varying outlooks, an older man than Job, one of his own age and a younger man, begin to argue with him and to reason with the sufferer, and the bulk of the Book after the Prologue, which we have studied already, is concerned with their arguments and his response or rather his continuing protests. As we see them arguing with Job, and as we watch Job wincing under the impact of their treatment, we notice something that we have no right ever to forget. These men, according to their lights, are treating Job correctly. Grant the premises from which they start and they are perfectly right in the way they handle him ; but we who know the real reason for his suffering can understand how they are simply adding to his misery. None of us would ever like to be called a Job's comforter, but all of us sooner or later are put in their position. We have to face up to somebody else who is bearing a very great burden of suffering ; we have to decide what we are going to say because we cannot keep silence for ever, and maybe in the strange providence of God all of us some day will have to face suffering for ourselves. So let us reckon with a reality which is clearly brought out by the attitude of Job's comforters and by his rather bitter response.

First let us recognise quite plainly that there is no theory of suffering that can cover every kind of suffering. In the day when this Book was written there was one theory that held the field. It covered everything, it supplied all the answers to every question in this vast and deep problem. It was the theory of retribution. All suffering of every kind came as a punishment for sin. Now that, originally, was a grand and inspiring idea, because it held the Jewish people when all the nations round about were worshipping strange gods who demanded the most unspeakable obscenities of their worshippers. The Jew clung to this, that we are living in a moral Universe that is governed by a righteous God, and you know where you are in it. You at least know this, that if you do wrong, you will pay for it. It was fundamentally a great, strong, inspiring idea, but the mistake was that they went on and drew the opposite conclusion. They said not only " if you sin you will suffer " ; they said " if you suffer then you must have sinned ". They started out with this one thought, this main theory, and they acted like the famous bandit in Greek mythology, Procrustes, who had a bed, and if he captured any victims on the highway he made them fit the bed. If they were not long enough he pulled them out until they fitted it, and if they were too long he chopped bits off until they fitted ! That is the way these good and well-meaning men treated this theory. They tried to make Job's situation fit into it. So Eliphaz begins by saying that of course since Job has suffered so much, he must have sinned grievously and if he will only confess his sin and repent, then God will relent and restore him. He cannot see that he is dealing with a really innocent man—with a man who will not deny his own integrity ; this is not just stubbornness on Job's part, it is his refusal to deny himself. Here is a kind of suffering that does not fit the bill—the theory does not explain it. That is true about any theory you may bring forward, concerning suffering ; it does not ever explain every kind of suffering.

Let us look at the modern equivalent of this theory. There are some rather extreme people holding this Christian faith of ours, and holding it quite sincerely, who maintain that everything that is wrong in the world to-day, all the suffering men have to face is the result, direct or indirect, of human sinfulness. In other words, we are paying all the time for living in a fallen world where man's rude work continually and everywhere defaces the paradise of God, or, as Paul put it, we are living in a set-up where " the whole creation groaneth and travaileth together ". There are even those who say that the very soil has turned sour because of the sin of man. All right—let us look at it. There is a lot to be said for it ; there is at least a proportion of real and challenging truth in it. For all the way from the Dust Bowl of America to the ploughed-up native tussock pastures of New Zealand, man's greed has exploited the soil and he has paid for it in the end. In one of the once lovely valleys of New Zealand, you can see a monstrosity that looks like a whole tenement block of buildings sitting in the middle of a river, moving a few inches at a time, moving just so many feet per day, chewing up and sucking into itself all that can be digested of the soil and silt and sand and stones from the bed of the river, extracting the few precious grains of the so-desirable gold, and leaving behind it nothing but piles of sterile gravel that will never grow anything. Yes, there is a reality in this. The greed and the sin of man have created situations for which we are all paying, and will go on paying for as long as we live. The sin of man is responsible for a very great deal of suffering.

In the kingdom of disease it is true also that human sin and ignorance have a very great deal to do with human suffering. Think of the slums of our great cities and what they do to the bodies and minds and souls of real people ; is not this suffering arising from a sinful human situation ? Or recall the problem described by A. J. Cronin in his autobiography where he tells of the little District Nurse fresh from her training, facing the first big epidemic of typhoid in the mining village of Tregenny, discovering that the Medical Officer just more or less took it for granted, accepting it as one of those things that happened periodically. But she was determined to fight this thing, surreptitiously taking samples of water from all the wells in the town, going off to Cardiff to get them analysed, pinning down the devil, the centre of infection, to the one well, having it closed and sealed off, and killing off the epidemic in a matter of days. What a lot of pain and suffering and misery and death is caused just by human ignorance or indolence or contentment with things just as they are ! This is obviously true, but it is not true far enough ; it does not have the whole answer ; it does not meet the worst kinds of suffering. Did the sin of man make the cruel sea as cruel as it is, with its terrifying power to smash and destroy and blot out of existence ? Did the sin of man make the very skin of the earth shudder, so that the earthquake does not scorn the just man to entomb, and the avalanche comes tumbling down the hillside to engulf men and women and innocent children—yes, innocent children ? This theory misses completely the terrific problem of the suffering of innocent people.

One of the great inescapable problems for anyone who regularly visits people in hospital, in these days when so many forms of disease have been conquered, is the suffering of so many very good people from the curse of cancer in one form or another. I think of the long, tragically long, list of people I have known over the years who were victims of this enemy. They would make up a list of some of the best and finest people I have ever known ; what they suffered could have no possible connection with anything they deserved, and therein lies the mystery. Of course, one realises that human sin comes in here again. Of course, it is obvious that if Great Britain and America had spent one hundredth part of the money they have poured out on armaments since World War II on research into cancer, they would almost certainly have found a real cure by now. One knows that, but it does not meet the difficulty. Why do such good people suffer so terribly ? One knows that they all have their share in the common burden of man's collective sin. We all have our share in it. It is no doubt true of these sufferers, in the words of the hymn

> " They who fain would serve Thee best
> Are conscious most of wrong within".

but it does not meet the case. There is no possible relation between what they suffer and what they deserve. Your theory is blown sky-high ; it does not meet that kind of suffering.

Nor does your test theory, the one that the Prologue suggests, that suffering is sent to test us, which it certainly does. But a test has meaning only if it can prove or demonstrate something, or if it can develop some latent power or possibility. These are the only circumstances in which a test has meaning. Have you ever seen a very young child in convulsion fits ? If you have, it is something you can never forget. It is horrible in the extreme, and what does it test ? The faith of the father and mother ? Yes, it tests that, but what in that struggling, unconscious little child does it test ? Have you ever seen someone driven out of his mind, past the point at which he loses his reason because of what he has had to suffer ? What does that prove or demonstrate or develop ? No, these theories are all very well, and to adduce them is right and proper, but there is no theory of suffering which covers every type of suffering that exists.

Then we remember, secondly, that there is no argument whatsoever that is not mocked by facts. Job's friends realise that their theory is not meeting with acceptance. They recognise that Job is not taking it too well, but they do not stop arguing. They realise that their arguments are not doing him any good, but they still go on arguing because we must. We must say what can be said ; we must do the little that can be done to justify the ways of God to men. They cannot realise that all their arguments are missing the main point of his suffering, which is not his physical misery, although that is extreme, and it is not his mental anguish, although that is almost unbearable, it is just that he feels that it is God who has done this to him, and he resents the cruelty and injustice of it all. All the arguments they bring are mocked by the man's own experience, and this is always true. Every argument we bring is mocked by the facts. Certainly we must say what can be said, and quite a lot can be said. For instance, we can say that many of the sufferings men and women have to endure are the reverse side of blessings we would never dream of doing without. Think of this terrible capacity for feeling pain. What is it but the reverse side of that wonderful blending of our senses that fills the world with beauty and with meaning ? It is the opposite side of the thing that enables the lover to thrill at the touch of his loved one's hand, and the two things must go together ; we cannot have the one without the other. You could put it in this way if you like, that pain is the discord in

" the mystic harmony
    Linking sense to sound and sight,"

as the hymn expresses it. The real pain of being a
man is just that we can remember and imagine, that
we look before and after and sigh for what is not.
And what are these things but the reverse side of
priceless gifts ? How awful it would be if we had no
memory ; if everything that happened just went as
soon as it was experienced, how poor we should be.
This capacity for remembering and feeling pain of
spirit is part of that. One knows this is true and this
can be said; but still the facts mock it.

Some of the powers in Nature that hurt us are just
the reverse side of powers that bless us—take fire, for
example. Some years ago there was a business man
in Edinburgh who had the ball at his feet, as the saying
goes. He had lots of money, he had a prosperous
position, he had a fine home and a wife and daughter,
both of whom he dearly loved. One evening he and
his wife on their way to a dance went to a friend's
house to pick up another couple and take them with
them in the car. While they waited the wife stood
for a moment beside an electric radiator in her filmy,
gauzy dance frock and went up in the twinkling of an
eye in a sheet of flame. They got her to hospital
where she died a few days later without regaining
consciousness. Well, the man was distracted, as you
can understand, but he tried to put life together
again. After a decent interval he married again for
the sake of his daughter. He drove himself, drove
himself, at his business just to try to forget, and after
a few months simply dropped dead in his tracks,
going out like a light. Now, could you possibly have
said to that man that fire was the thing that drove his
business, the motive power of his construction lorries
and bulldozers and the rest, the driving power of his
great enterprises, the same thing that killed his wife ?
No ! Not when you were mocked by that charred,

unrecognisable thing that had been a lovely, laughing woman. The facts mock your argument.

You can argue if you will, and you will argue rightly, that God had to take a risk, that God took the greatest of all risks when He entrusted us with the perilous gift of free-will. If we were to be free to say " yes " we had to be free to say " no ". If we were to be free to obey, we were also free to disobey. If we were to be free to heal, we must be free to hurt. God had to take the risk, and on the whole, surely, it was worth it. But here is a man after a convivial evening, getting ready for going home. He says he will just take " one for the road ", takes it and goes out and starts up his car, monarch of all he surveys, sitting on top of his world. He drives a few yards along the street and overtakes a stationary bus, from which just at the stop there is jumping a laughing girl with her skating boots slung over her shoulder, waving farewell to her chums, saying when she will meet them again. Because his reactions are just that tiny shade more sluggish, he does not stop in time, and they pick up from under his front wheel—no not a dead girl, it might have been better so—but a girl so injured that she is paralysed from the waist down and she will never walk again. She will never put on again the skating boots that are lying there sprawled across the street ; she will never marry, she will never fulfil her woman's destiny of having a family of her own. Are you going to say to that girl or her mother that God was justified in taking the risk of giving us free-will ? No, the arguments are all of them mocked by the facts.

So we are driven inevitably and necessarily and rightly to this, that you cannot argue with a tragedy. Job's comforters, notorious as they now are, just could not see it. They were trying to argue with a tragedy, and arguments, right or wrong, were utterly out of place. What this man needed was something to help him to hold on to God. He did not want arguments and theories, he wanted somebody to take his struggling hand and link it to the hand of God. Nothing less than that would do any good at all. He was trying desperately to keep hold on God himself, and they were not helping him in the least.

Let us never forget that, in all our theorizing about the problem of suffering. You cannot ever argue with a real tragedy. The only thing that does any good, the only thing that matters in the very least, is that you should somehow give to that person who is suffering a sense of the power and presence of God—just enough to keep holding on ; not any all-embracing solution, with all the answers neatly docqueted, but just enough to keep holding on. We all know how difficult it is. When did you last try to write a letter of condolence to somebody, either in bereavement or in personal suffering ? Did you write easily and glibly ? Well, if you did, you should not have written it, for it ought not to be that way. When did you last go into a home where someone was in sheer agony of body, mind or spirit ? What did you say ? Did words trip easily to your tongue ? Better to have bitten your tongue than let that happen, for the only thing that matters is just somehow to let the sufferer be sure of God. Yes, even if it is only to be sure in the way Job had to be when he cried out : " Though he slay me, yet will I trust him ". If he can hold on to that, that is enough. The Guider in charge of the Trefoil School for Cripple Children recently spoke about this problem of suffering to three " practitioners " in suffering, girls who had been in the school for a long time and who never were utterly free from pain. She said to them : " When do you feel most sure of God ? " Two of them said that it was when the suffering was worst. What a challenge ! It was when the suffering was worst that they felt nearest to God. The third girl said it was not like that with her. When the suffering passed, there was such a wonderful sense of relief that her gratitude made her feel closer to God. But these three girls, quite young girls, conquered this thing because they still felt close to God.

The great Dr. Jowett tells of a man whom he visited regularly, and who was dying of cancer, in the throat of all places. As time passed, he became quite incapable of speech, and his minister visiting him had to do all the speaking, but the man used now and then to take a pad of paper and write something on it. The last day he was conscious and able to reply to the words of comfort spoken by the minister, he signed that he wanted the paper tablet and the pencil. Laboriously he printed something on it and then lay back exhausted on the pillows. What had he written ? " Bless the Lord, O my soul, and forget not all His benefits ". He had found the only thing that mattered, the only thing that could help ; he had kept his hold on God in spite of everything. Surely there is a heartening challenge here to those among us who ourselves have suffered. If you have known real suffering in any degree yourself, you have a duty. You have a duty to do what lies in your power to help somebody else in like suffering, for the only argument worth bringing forward, the only word we sometimes dare to speak at all, is to say with the Psalmist : " I was brought low, and he helped me."

4

THE RIGHT TO COMPLAIN

" My soul is weary of my life ; I will leave my complaint upon
myself ; I will speak in the bitterness of my soul."—Job x. 1.

MORE than thirty years ago when I was *en route*
to study in Zürich University, I found myself,
with several hours to fill in, in the city of Basle ; for
want of anything better to do I went into a cinema,
which was a rather foolish thing to do considering
that I then knew practically no German. The film
happened to be the story of Dreyfus, the French
officer who was twice condemned for treason and then
finally completely exonerated and acquitted ; and
even the English-speaking spectator was able to follow,
at least the trend of the story, however imperfectly.

One scene from that film stood out and remains
indelibly printed on my memory. It was when this
man, knowing himself to be innocent, had been condemned as guilty and was being led away from the
Court-room ; as he was being hustled off between his
captors, he kept on crying out in German (it was, of
course, a film for a German-speaking audience) " *Ich
bin unschuldig, ich bin unschuldig, ich bin unschuldig* ".
Now, although one member of the audience knew no
German he still understood perfectly what the man
was saying. I realised that here was a protest boiling
up from the man's very soul and it was not to be
silenced ; they could do nothing to stop him protesting
his innocence, and that is precisely what is happening
at this stage in the developing drama of Job.

The friends of Job are shocked and horrified at his
reaction to his suffering and they are doing their level
best to silence him. They are rather like men who
try, ineffectively, to stun some sufferer into senseless-

ness. They beat him about the head with the belabour-
ing of their blundering arguments, but still they
cannot silence him ; he still maintains his right to
protest first of all against their inability to understand
and then, greatly daring, to protest to God Himself.
The next few chapters of this strange Book are full of
Job's appeal away from the men who cannot understand, direct to God Himself. So Job at this stage is
asserting and maintaining his right to complain.

It will be remembered that the whole purpose of this
series of studies is to try to discover not only the right
way of thinking about suffering but also right ways of
handling it. We have now reached the stage when we
must stop and ask : " What is the right reaction to
suffering ? "

First it must be recognised quite simply and plainly
that if the teaching of this Book means anything, then
it means that it is part of our human destiny to assert
our right to complain. That may seem, at first sight,
quite startling and even directly wrong. It is important
to explain precisely what is meant by this statement.
There are many different attitudes which real people
in actual practice adopt when suffering comes either
to them or to their loved ones. There is the attitude
of stoic fortitude. Fortitude and courage are not the
same thing ; courage may lead up to fortitude, but
fortitude has an enduring quality about it that is not
necessarily present in some sudden, swift act of
courage. The classic expression of that kind of fortitude is in Henley's poem.

> " In the fell clutch of circumstance,
> I have not winced nor cried aloud ;
> Under the bludgeonings of chance
> My head is bloody, but unbowed."

That is the kind of fortitude with which some people
manage to face suffering, and it is quite amazing how
general that is, even in people with no vestige of
Christian faith. World War II wrote story after story

of people, both in the Services and in " civvy street ",
who faced terrible suffering with amazing fortitude.
This can be illustrated again and again. Go back once
more to A. J. Cronin, to his dramatic story of his first
accident in the pit ; how he crawled in beside a man
who was trapped, his foot crushed and held by the
weight of rock from the roof, with the roof still cracking
and likely to fall at any moment. The only chance of
getting the man out was to amputate the trapped leg
as quickly as possible below the knee. He told the
man what he was going to do, gave him the anaesthetic
as best he could in that cramped situation and started
the amputation. When he was just about to saw
through the bone of the leg, there was a slight splinter-
ing of the roof and a stone fell and smashed the bottle
with the ether in it, but he had to go on with his work.
As he finished the last piece of stitching to that terrible
wound, he looked up and saw the eyes of the patient
open, dilated with pain, watching him. The man's
voice said without a tremor : " You've made a good
job of it, doctor, bach. I only saw the hint end of it,
but you've made a good job ". The man had been
out of the anaesthetic for the last five minutes and had,
quite literally, " neither winced nor cried aloud ".
Now that is great ; that kind of fortitude is a wonderful
reaction to suffering, but at its best it is only a negative
refusal to be conquered by suffering.

The next attitude we might notice is that of Christian
resignation, which is not quite the same thing. We
might illustrate this by the reaction of the father of
Richard Cameron, the Covenanting preacher, when he
was imprisoned in the Tolbooth of Edinburgh. They
came to him one day, and out of a sack they rolled
something in front of him—the severed head and
hands of a man. He looked at them and he said :
" It is the head and hands of Richard. It is the will of
the Lord ; good is the will of the Lord." In other
words, here was a tragedy simply to be accepted, for
the will of the Lord was inscrutable and we must not

even start to question it or seek to understand. Again
that is great ; of course, it can degenerate into a kind
of fatalism, but it is great because it is a practical way
of handling suffering. You can take it, if you take it
this way, but it is still a negative reaction.

Then there is the attitude of Job, and we must look
carefully to discern what his attitude is, and what it
is not. It is not a mere complaining of his personal
hurt. This is no mere crying out : " Why did God
have to do this to me ? "—an all-too-common reaction
to suffering. This is not just a general " girning "
against life ; it is a cry wrung from the depths of the
man's very being and as such it deserves to be taken
very seriously. Where does such a cry come from in
the end—when a man appeals to God against God,
which is what it amounts to—when this protest comes
from his very soul and cannot be silenced ? Where is
such a cry coming from in the last resort ? There is
a well-known line from Burns which gives us the clue :

> " Who made the heart, 'tis He alone
> Decidedly can try us."

Surely it is not fanciful to suggest that this kind of
protest comes from God Himself, it is God who put it
into us to take suffering that way, at times. It is part
of the pain of being a man that we must have this
complaint deep down in our very souls.

In Dorothy Sayers' play, *The Zeal of Thine House*,
there is a very striking passage where the two angels
are discussing a situation and one of them says :
" Why ? " Immediately the other cuts in and says :
" No, angels don't ask Why, only mortals ask Why."
It seems to be part of our human destiny to ask
" Why ? " If God made us to ask " Why ? ", to
complain in such a situation, then it is wrong to pretend
that it is not so. It is wrong to crush this down where
it will do us even more harm, if the psychologists are
right, but it is wrong for a deeper reason still. We
simply cannot go on thinking about this whole dark

problem as if we were not seeing it, all the time, in the light shed upon it by the Cross. And when we look at the Cross, we are being allowed to eavesdrop, as it were, on a dark, deep, and sacred mystery. For there was One other Who cried : " My God, Why ? " We suggest, then, that to reserve the right to complain is part of our human destiny.

Now we can go on to look at the nature of Job's complaint, which is also our own. It is a complaint first and foremost about lack of justice. This goes very deep in our human nature. You will find it, most pronounced, in a little child, as most of us very well know. If you accuse a child wrongly of something that child has not done, you may, as some have done, beat that child almost insensible, to compel him to confess. He will still cry out : " It isn't fair, I didn't do it "—" *Ich bin unschuldig* ". It is because this sense of justice goes right down to the very roots of our being that when we feel a thing is wrong we must protest, and that is why Job is complaining first of all. It is wrong ; he is an innocent man punished as if he were guilty, and he will not take it uncomplaining. Wherever we, too, see injustice at the heart of suffering, we ought to complain.

The Hindu explains the problem of suffering in his doctrine of Karma, which is retribution for something I did in a previous incarnation, when I was not recognisably myself, but where that life was linked to this. So a Hindu can say of Jesus : " He must have been a terrible sinner in a previous incarnation, He was such a terrible sufferer in this life ". It is wrong ! Where is the justice in my being punished for something I am supposed to have done when I was not " I ", where there is no sense of link and conscience and continuity between the two ? It's wrong, it won't do. It is wrong that a child should suffer for the sins of its parents, and children do so suffer. We all know there are children born blind and handicapped because of the sins of their parents, and something deep within us cries : " It is wrong, it ought not to be ". It is wrong that children anywhere suffer as they do so often, as they do, for example, in war. Now, war in itself is not conclusive evidence of any injustice on the part of God. If men and nations could behave the way they do and no war come, it would be a bigger evidence of an immoral universe than all the evils of war itself, and let us not forget it. But it is because war causes such suffering to children who, in any age or generation and of any race or side are innocent—it is because war causes that, that we say this thing is wrong. It is the injustice of it that sears the conscience.

We cry out : " Why is it that suffering in quantity and quality is so ill-distributed ? Why do some folk have to bear so much and others get off scot-free ? Why four drowned children in one family ? Why four, why all of them ? " This is the kind of question that haunts us and lays hold upon our minds and hearts. Nor is it merely a matter of the quantity of such suffering. Is that loss in a drowning accident four times as terrible as the loss of an only child ? We know it is not a matter of simple arithmetic. It is the quality of suffering and unjust suffering that haunts our heart ; for why is it that the finer the person the greater seems the capacity for suffering ? Why is it that such good people have so much given them to bear ? We cry out against the injustice of suffering, and we are right so to do. So out of this first part of Job's complaint comes this—whatever solution we seek and find for the problem of suffering, it must make room, it must give time for justice to be done or at least vindicated. And we know, we who are reading this story, we know that justice *is* done. We have seen it from the level above. We know perfectly well that God is not punishing an innocent man unjustly ; He is testing him unbearably ; He is trusting him almost intolerably, but there is no injustice when you know the whole story.

There is a particular " parlour game " which is

becoming increasingly popular at family parties on a reasonable scale. It consists of a series of odd photographs of quite familiar objects, taken from an unusual angle, which the players are supposed to identify. It may be something like a door-key seen end-on, or a garden trowel photographed with nothing but the handle towards you ; for the life of you, you cannot tell what these odd objects are because you are not seeing them from the right angle ; you do not recognise them and cannot understand what they are meant to be. Maybe that is why so much suffering looks unjust to us. We, seeing it from our angle, cannot recognise it for what it is and for what God meant it to be. So we cry out concerning lack of justice.

The second part of Job's complaint and our own is a complaint concerning lack of purpose. Job is bursting out in protest against the explanations that his friends give. He will not have it that he is being punished for secret sin because he keeps on protesting his innocence, yet he must try to explain it all the same. He must try to arrive at his own answer and in seeking it he is utterly bewildered by one fact. Why has God previously been so good to him ? Why did He give him all this prosperity, his seven sons and three daughters, if He meant from the beginning only to wipe them out ? To Job that does not make sense and it does not make sense to us either.

Why is there this apparent non-sense about life with this element of suffering ? Why does it not fit in and show a purpose ? Put it like this. Does it make sense that God should give to a woman like Kathleen Ferrier her golden voice, capable of giving not only intense pleasure, but infinite enrichment to those who hear her, just in order, far too soon, to muffle that voice by pain and weakness and then silence it for ever ? It does not make sense. Why does God allow a man with the surgeon's co-ordination of hand and mind and heart to develop a skill of his own, to spend it without any guarding of his strength,

and then make these hands wasted and useless and in
the end laid aside for ever ? It does not make sense.
In our hearts we cry out that there should be a purpose
even in suffering. Even if we cannot see it, as long as
we can believe that it is there we can go on. We
know, of course, that there are by-products of suffering
described like this in the familiar poem : -

" The cry of earth's anguish went up to God,
   ' Lord, take away pain from the world
Thou hast made, that it love Thee the more '.
   Then answered the Lord to the world He had made,
' Shall I take away pain and with it the power of the
     soul
   To endure, made strong by the strain ?
Shall I take away love that redeems with a price
   And smiles through the loss ?
Can you spare from the lives that would climb up to
   Mine
     The Christ on His Cross ? ' "

We all know that there do exist such wonderful
by-products of suffering, but it still cannot silence our
cry that suffering ought to mean something, and if we
can go on believing that, if we saw it from the proper
angle, and in the light of the whole truth, it would
mean something understandable, then we can go on
facing it. Yes, even if this also is inescapably true:

" Not until the loom is silent,
   and the shuttles cease to fly,
Will God unroll the canvas,
   and explain the reason why ;
How the dark threads are as needful
   in the weaver's skilful hand,
As the threads of gold and silver,
   in the pattern he has planned."

But our every instinct still insists that there should be
a pattern.
Complaint of lack of justice, complaint of lack of
purpose, and finally, and by far the worst of all, complaint of lack of love. That is what makes Job so

bitter and that is what so often deeply embitters us—
it looks as if God simply did not care. It does not
matter to Him that we have to face this, and that
those we love have to bear this. It matters not at all
to Him—He does not seem to care. Job, struggling,
striving, complaining, trying to get through to God,
appealing to God against God, as it were, is expressing
something that sooner or later we all understand.

How tragic it is if God should prove to be quite
inaccessible. One of the great passages in Scott's
novels is the description in *The Heart of Midlothian* of
Jeannie Deans and her desperate journey to London
to plead with the Queen for her sister's life. What a
wonderful description is given of how she goes and
throws herself, not without dignity, upon the pity and
mercy of the Queen and is successful. Terrible if we
cannot do that with God, if there is no journey we
can take that will get us home to Him and gain us a
hearing. Tragic if there is nothing we can do to make
God feel what this means to us. That is where there
is a wonderful and inspired bit of prophecy in Job.
In the chapter before this he said " neither is there any
daysman betwixt us, that might lay his hand upon us
both ". Now the daysman was an umpire, an arbiter,
somebody with authority who stood between two
contesting parties, and held them together and wrought
out a solution that would satisfy them both. What a
wonderful fore-glimpse and fore-taste of what Jesus
Christ alone has done ! Here at last is someone to
take suffering humanity by the hand, and with
authority—the authority of experience—let God understand what it is like to suffer our way, to struggle in
the dark and cry out, " My God, why ? " And then
on the other hand, quite literally on the other hand,
to take hold of God and make real to suffering humanity
the justice, the purpose and the love in which it is so
terribly hard at times to go on believing.

So you see we have come by the way of this complaint that might seem wrong and yet ought not to be

silenced, we have come to the stage of seeing what the answer ought to be, if it is to satisfy both mind and heart. Thank God, we all know we have come to what the answer *is*. In *Rab and his Friends* the doctor writing the story gives one illustration of how this answer has been found, when he describes the country carrier's wife brought in for operation. Without wincing or crying aloud, with no anaesthetic whatever, she suffered the removal of a breast. Although she died after the operation he gives an immortal description of what she was like, and the feature in it that matters is this, that her eyes were full of pain and sorrow, " but full also of the overcoming ". What a wonderful overcoming has been made possible because there is a Daysman now between suffering man and a loving God.

5

GLEAMS OF LIGHT IN THE DARKNESS

" I know that my redeemer liveth."—Job xix. 25.

WE have now reached the stage in our study of the problem of suffering when certain facts are becoming quite plain and there are three which belong together and each of which develops out of the other.

The first fact which is quite unmistakable at this stage is that suffering looks quite different, depending upon whether you are viewing it from the inside or from the outside. There is a great phrase which is born of Job's suffering and which glows with meaning and reality. He says, " If your soul were in my soul's stead, I could heap up words against you ". In other words, if they could change places, the person standing outside and comfortably theorising, and the suffering soul, in the middle of the suffering, agonising, the problem would look quite different. Maybe that fact will teach us all a certain degree of humility and reverence in dealing with a sufferer or in thinking about suffering. Certainly it makes this quite plain, that there is a great difference between suffering seen from the inside and suffering viewed in the abstract, and that realisation ought to bring us immediately to recognise the inadequacy of any theorising whatsoever. In fact, it looks as if in order to get a true picture we should take the witness of people who, speaking out of the heart of the problem, can speak with an undeniable authority. There died a short time ago in one of our Edinburgh hospitals a man aged seventy-two, and it was simply noted in the death notice, as if it were not specially significant, that he had been in that hospital for fifty-four years. He entered it a boy of eighteen,

48

he died as a man of seventy-two ; he had spent almost all the years of this century in a hospital for incurables and if out of that he could tell us what suffering looks like, we might be coming nearer to reality. If along with him we could get the witness of someone like, shall we say, Odette Churchill, someone who has suffered actual torture, deliberately inflicted for an evil purpose, if we could see what that looks like from the receiving end, then we might begin to know something about it. Or if, without being so dramatic, we could simply draw on any one of the many possible sufferers, people who have endured, shall we say, rheumatoid arthritis for more years than they care to count, where they have always been in pain, night and day, waking and sleeping, though sometimes the pain has been worse than others ; if somebody out of that experience could give evidence we might know where we are and most of our theorising would prove to be completely irrelevant.

Anyhow we come to this, that in studying the experience of Job it now becomes quite plain that if there is to be any answer at all it must come from the sufferer himself. He is getting no help from his friends and we shall not get any help there either. He appeals to them in vain ; he turns to God and gets no response. If there is to be any answer whatsoever it has to come out of the man himself, and that is exactly what we now see happening.

Just as a diamond is made, not by any easy process but by great heat and under great pressure, just as it can be made only in that way and not synthetically, because if anyone did succeed in making it synthetically it would have neither the glow nor the lustre of one made in Nature's own fire ; so out of Job's own experience, out of his sheer desperation and misery, under the pressure of it there is struck off from his own life every here and there a spark of light, a gleam of fire, as it were, which lightens the darkness of this problem. As in an old village smithy the dark dusty corners are illumined when the smith takes the glowing metal in his tongs and lays it on the anvil, and beats it cruelly with his hammer, so sparks of truth and gleams of light come to us for our enlightening, struck off from Job's experience. What then are they ?

First of all, out of the depth and darkness of his misery Job comes to the astonishing idea of God yearning after His own creature. In order to discover and to follow the development of his thought, we must realise afresh how total was Job's darkness. You see, first of all he was incurable ; remember that about leprosy, it was quite incurable, there was no glimmer of hope anywhere. He has become loathsome, as he tells us, to his own wife, to his friends and to himself. He is utterly degraded and completely disgraced and all about him is total blank darkness— no light anywhere—and what makes it worst of all is that God is doing this. He is cut off from God, he cannot make God hear, he cannot bring any kind of plea to God ; he knows that he is going to die and that when he dies it will be too late. What tragedy and pathos run through the chapter from which this text is taken ! When a man dies it is too late, and Job pictures himself going down into that dim world of shades which is no existence at all and where not even God can reach and help a man. Did you ever realise that it is Job who gives immortal voice to that age-long, ever-repeated cry of the human heart : " If a man die shall he live again ? " He cries that cry because he knows only one answer, the empty answer " no ", and having uttered that cry, all of a sudden he leaps out of the darkness and speaks for himself, hearing God call, even after he is dead, and answering because God has begun to yearn for the work of His hands. Now that is a great thought, or rather it is the beginning of a great thought. Here is Job thinking of God as being like, shall we say, a potter who has lavished his skill, skill coming from his brain down through his sensitive, clever fingers, upon some priceless vase. Now he sees it broken into fragments, but he cannot leave it like that. Because he created it he must piece it together again and as far as he may restore it. Or as a painter, looking at a canvas on which he once set down a dream, a vision of his own mind and heart, seeing it blistered by fire or mouldering with damp, must do something about it because he yearns after the work of his hands ; so Job pictures God yearning after him. It is a great thought with a tremendous truth at its heart, because it is leading on to the thought of the father yearning after his child. When Principal Sir George Adam Smith, that great Hebrew scholar, was in Aberdeen he told how once a trawler skipper shared with him an experience that was very revealing. He described how in a terrible storm in the North Sea he had been standing on the deck of his little ship with his son beside him when a great wave without any warning swept over the trawler. The father managed to hold on in time but the son was swept away before his eyes, and he said : " For one awful minute which seemed like an eternity I saw my son there in the trough of the wave, crying out with a voice I could not hear for help I was powerless to give, and then the waves sucked him under. And then ", said the trawler skipper, " for the first time I knew what the Psalmist meant when he said ' Like as a father pitieth his children, so the Lord pitieth them that fear him ' ". Go back to two pictures we used earlier, to the mother of the burned child yearning to take the hurt into herself, to the husband by the bedside of his sick wife, yearning to put his strength into her weakness; this is the way in which Job is beginning to picture God ; he is beginning to lead us in the direction of singing " O Love that wilt not let me go " because there is a love that yearns for us and cannot let us go. So Job has helped us with his gleam of light. You see, whatever we may have to suffer and however wrong it may seem, it does not mean—if this is true—it does not mean that

God has grown callous and unheeding. It does mean that whatever else may happen God yearns with an incurable longing for His children and He just cannot let them go. Job did not clearly see this himself ; he had his gleam of light and then he was enveloped in darkness again, but we can see it. Alexander Whyte of Free St. George's once said : " Many a time I feel so cold and dead that I might doubt if I had ever come to Him at all, but I go about my work notwithstanding, looking in His direction ". Job did not see for himself the Love that will not let us go, but he was at least looking in His direction.

Then, secondly, we find Job appealing from God to God. He is on the horns of an intolerable dilemma because, at one and the same time, he feels the cruelty of what has happened, he is burdened with the bitter injustice of it all, and yet he still believes in the love and justice of God. How in all the world is he to put the two together ? It is almost as if there were two sides to God's character and Job is appealing to the one against the other, as if God were two people in one. So we find Job next crying out, wishing somebody could be a witness for him in Heaven, somebody who could be surety for him with God, somebody, if you will forgive the phrase, to " go bail " for him before God, and he finds himself driven into the incredible position of recognising that only God could do that. Nobody could possibly be his witness in Heaven except God Himself. The beauty of it is that we know that this is the right answer. We have been let into the secret beforehand ; we can understand the whole story, and we know that Job is gloriously right. In the Council of Heaven it is God Himself who stands up for Job, who boasts about him, is proud of him, and never loses His faith in him. Job has got at the right answer through the darkness. So we find ourselves confronted by Job with this quite impossible yet entirely realistic situation that God is at one and the same time evidently and obviously unjust, and

still justice itself. He allows or He sends cruel suffering,
yet He is still love at heart. William Cowper has
taught us to sing, in old-fashioned phrase, " behind a
frowning providence He hides a smiling face ", a
statement which often seems not to make sense, but
it is still truth. Job has come to know now that God
has at least not forgotten, God has not deserted him,
God has in Himself a witness to Job and He never can
forget.

We take this for granted because we have Christian
truth to support it, but it is not to be taken for granted.
The awful alternative is starkly expressed in Thomas
Hardy's bitter poem *God Forgotten* :—

" I towered far, and lo ! I stood within
   The presence of the Lord Most High,
Sent thither by the sons of Earth, to win
       Some answer to their cry.

' The Earth, sayest thou ? The Human race ?
By Me created ? Sad its lot ?
Nay : I have no remembrance of such place :
       Such world I fashioned not.'

' O Lord, forgive me when I say
Thou spakest the word, and madest it all.'—
' The Earth of men . . . let me bethink me. . . . Yea !
       I dimly do recall

' Some tiny sphere I built long back
(Mid millions of such shapes of mine)
So named. . . . It perished, surely—not a wrack
       Remaining, or a sign ?

' It lost my interest from the first,
My aims therefor succeeding ill ;
Haply it died of doing as it durst ? '
       ' Lord, it existeth still'. "

That could never happen, that can never be the
awful truth because God has gone out of His way, of
His own accord, to give us a surety for Himself.

Another hymn writer has set this truth to poetry, for it cannot be kept to pedestrian prose :—

> " There is a way for man to rise
>   To that sublime abode :
> An offering and a sacrifice,
> A Holy Spirit's energies,
>   An Advocate with God."

There is your witness in Heaven. We sing our way, further, to the heart of this wonderful mystery :—

> " The Saviour dy'd, but rose again
>   triumphant from the grave ;
> And pleads our cause at God's right hand,
>   omnipotent to save."

> " Our fellow-suff'rer yet retains
> A fellow-feeling of our pains ;
> And still remembers in the skies
> His tears, his agonies, and cries."

We cannot ever say to God, now, bitterly, " ' If your soul were in my soul's stead ' things would be different in this suffering world ". No, Job has not seen the whole way to that, but he is at least moving in that direction.

So he comes, and so he leads us with him, to the greatest inspiration of all, to that tremendous flash of imaginative faith which Christian thought ever since has insisted on interpreting as the first gleam of the glorious dawn : " I know that my redeemer liveth ". Just because these words are so familiar, just because they are all coloured with associations we must be very careful here. You see, what matters is not what the words mean to us now, but what did they mean to Job. The word " redeemer " is very misleading because it certainly did not mean to Job what it means to you and me, someone who delivers us from every enemy, including, first and foremost, sin ; it means, fundamentally, someone who vindicates your good name. Moffatt's translation " champion " is perhaps

as near as we can get to it. Now look at Job, going
down he believes to the total darkness of the grave
in misery and disgrace, crying out, " Still I know
One to champion me at the last, to stand up for me
on the earth over my dust ". " After I am dead and
gone," he says, " there will still be One, a living
champion of all I have believed in." That would be
great enough in itself, but now—the flash coming
from nowhere, out of nothing but his suffering, the
sheer inspiration of it—he goes beyond that and he
cries, " Yes, after I am dead, after the worms destroy
this body, after my flesh has mouldered from my
bones, I shall still come back and I shall see myself
vindicated ; I shall see God for myself and not
another ". What a wonderful faith, what an amazing
inspiration ! Yet it leaves us thinking and wondering,
what if that were all ? This, after all, is only the
first pale glimmering of the light of belief in a general
resurrection.   Someone   among   the   commentators
(these clever people) declares : " This is only an
ad hoc resurrection ", that is to say a resurrection
specially for this one limited purpose, there is not in
it yet the glory of life eternal. Not quite yet—but
the possibility is here, and as we read it and think :
" Well, if that were all, how poor we should be ", we
thank God that it is not all. Did you ever notice
that in these immortal words of Job set to the music
from Handel's *Messiah*, words and music wedded
for ever, there is a mistake, a mis-quotation ? Handel
is absolutely right, he is supremely inspired when he
takes these words of Job and sets them down, " I
know that my redeemer liveth and though worms
destroy this body, yet in my flesh shall I see God ",
and then he gives the reason, " For now is Christ
risen ". But that is not the correct quotation from
i Cor. xv. ; it should be " *but* now is Christ risen ",
only Handel sees that the " but " would be wrong.
It is the " for " that is right, since it is only when
Job's flash of inspiration is caught up into the full

daylight of the Resurrection that its meaning becomes
plain. " I know that my redeemer liveth, for now is
Christ risen."

It is a pity that it is so hard for us to grasp the full
difference that has been made. At the Funeral Service
in St. Giles' Cathedral of the late Duke of Montrose
the choir sang most beautifully and movingly Tennyson's *Crossing the Bar*. Yes, you can sing these familiar
words, you can listen to them, and they can move your
heart :

> " Twilight and evening bell,
> And after that the dark ? "

You can listen to these words without any incurable
" sadness of farewell " because you know it is not total
dark, and never will be again. You can listen to it
because the dark has light at its heart for ever.

There is a Champion. Just as in *Ivanhoe* when
Rebecca is left to her fate, with nobody to stand up
for her, at the last minute a champion comes riding
into the lists, so this poor, battered, blundering,
bewildered, suffering humanity of ours has found a
new Champion. The horizons of life are pushed back
and back, and this is not any more the only life with
which we are concerned. If it were, this problem of
suffering would be quite intolerable ; it would be
incredibly unjust and unbearably cruel. But now we
can say : " I reckon that the sufferings of this present
time are not worthy to be compared with the glory
which shall be revealed ". Job did not see that ; he
had only this one brilliant, incomparable flash of light
which we have taken up and developed. He fell back
again for the time into his own darkness, but where for
Job there was only the gleam, thank God, for us there
is the Glory. We can say, not only as Job said, but
with a new wealth of meaning : " I know that my
Redeemer liveth ".

6

GOD'S OWN RESPONSE

" Then the Lord answered Job out of the whirlwind."—Job
xxxviii. 1.

" I have heard of thee by the hearing of the ear : but now mine
eye seeth thee."—Job xlii. 5.

WE have called this final study " God's Own
Response ", but we should have gone on to
add " and Job's Reaction ". Certainly both belong
together, and both are equally surprising. In one of
the lovely singing chapters of Isaiah God is represented
as saying to His people : " My thoughts are not your
thoughts, neither are your ways my ways ". The
writer of the Book of Job has clearly caught and quite
startlingly illustrated that truth. When he brings us
to his own solution of the problem of suffering it is not
at all in the way we should expect or think likely. As
the drama moves on we are made ever more acutely
aware of the hopeless dilemma in which Job finds
himself. He becomes more and more conscious of the
deep injustice of his lot and increasingly disappointed
at the complete failure of his friends to understand
his attitude or to offer any real comfort. In the later
speeches they merely reiterate the old stock arguments
and become more direct and brutal in their allegations
of secret sin. Job keeps repeating his indictment of
God for unheeding cruelty and gross injustice, and
insists on reasserting his integrity and protesting his
innocence in the sublime thirty-first chapter. He
ends by crying on God with pathetic eagerness to
condescend to meet him, to tell him the nature of his
offence, to break silence and answer his appeal. Surely
God must respond if there is any God who hears and
answers prayer !

Several years ago there stood among the trees above the Clyde valley near Lanark a burned-out mansion house. It had been completely gutted in an all-engulfing conflagration and stood now an empty shell of bare blackened walls. But as you walked round among the ruins you noticed that the brass bell-handle was still in its place at the side of the doorway. If you went and pulled it, to your complete surprise the bell still rang in the heart of the dead and empty house. It rang with a weird and hollow mockery in such a place. Unless the deepest agonising cries of the human heart mean no more than that, pulling a bell that rings in the heart of a dead and empty universe where there is no one to answer, then God must respond to such an agonising cry as this of Job. God does answer, but it is all utterly different from what we should expect. God will be very gentle, we think ; He will come in healing peace, dropping His still dews of quietness on the tortured mind and heart and soul of the sufferer. God does nothing of the kind. He answers Job " out of the whirlwind ". He comes, it seems, not to answer but to overpower. He over-whelms this despairing man with a sense of the divine greatness and the insignificance of human life till He humbles him into dumb silence. If the friends of Job bludgeoned him with their blundering arguments, God repeatedly strikes him down with the weapon of His irony. " You, who deign to criticize ", He says, " you who accuse me of mismanagement and injustice . . . where were you when the foundations of the earth were laid, when the morning stars sang together, and all the sons of God shouted for joy ? " In a brilliant, glittering kaleidoscope of unparalleled poetry God spreads before Job the mystery of sea and earth, rain, snow, ice, stars and clouds. Then follows a colourful parade of the living creatures, the wild goat, ass, unicorn, ostrich, horse (a wonderful description, vibrant with life), hawk and eagle. All combine to produce a demonstration of the majesty and mystery of creation before which man can only bow in abject humility. Then the thought is carried, cruelly it seems, a stage further still. " You criticise My ordering of the life of the world. Come then ! Change places with Me. You take control and run the world, you make life better, fairer, more kind and just. You overthrow the wicked, whose success you take so much to heart. You cast down the proud who lord it over the good. You put an end to all the evils to which you take such bitter objection. Then when you have handled all the world, with its problems, so much better than I do, I will applaud and tell you how well you have done ! " That is no answer at all, unless it is an answer to be told that you have no right to ask questions, no cause to complain ; yes, unless it is an answer to be reminded of your utter ignorance, and of that baffling inability to understand which is already your torment. Yet the strange thing is that Job seems to feel he *is* answered, he has found the response for which his heart has craved. He admits before God his ignorance and presumption, but with the air of one who in some strange way has come to know all he needs to know on earth. He has found rest and peace in a new kind of knowledge. Formerly he knew God only by hearsay, now he has " seen " God.

What are we to take out of all this, so bewilderingly different from what we should expect, that can be helpful in that right thinking about suffering and in that victorious handling of it which have been our great aims throughout this whole study ?

One of the first needs of any man facing suffering at first hand is to be lifted out of himself as God so forcibly lifted Job. Naturally, understandably, perhaps inevitably Job is concerned most of all with himself ; in that sense he is self-centred. He may arraign the general injustice of God's handling of His world, but it is the injustice to himself that really matters. He accuses God of being cruel and unheeding

to far too many of His children, but it is the cruelty
he is suffering that rankles. As his friends, with their
obtuseness, increasingly fail him, he becomes more
and more shut up in a little world bounded by his own
suffering, where the whole sky is shadowed by his
personal darkness, where the only realities are his
pain, his misery, his degradation, his despair. That
still happens, and only those who have never known
that experience can fail to appreciate it. You have
lain in that tiny world of the sick room so long ; you
have counted the very flowers on the wallpaper until
you are nearly driven mad by the counting ; you have
stared at that ceiling until the very fly-marks are
completely familiar ; you have waited for the return
of pain, pain like an animal crouching in the darkness
waiting to pounce on its victim. You have longed—
how you have longed—for the merciful drugged
oblivion of induced sleep, yet when it came it took the
mind wandering in strange and terrible places from
which you were glad to return. That alone is real to
you, the universe for you centres round that, even
God matters only in so far as you can relate Him to
that. When that happens there is nothing so important
as to be lifted out of that situation.

Until a few years ago there lived in the village of
Darvel, in the Irvine valley of Ayrshire, a man whom
the casual visitor never saw but whom those who
were taken to see him greatly admired. You were
ushered into a sick room, small and rather dark and
dull, with the door opening on to the bed. The invalid
lay in the dark corner behind the door, away from
the window, outside of which were the light and air
and life of the village square and all the movement of
the wider world. That man had lain there for forty-
two years ! But he had never been a " shut-in " for
on the window by the foot of the bed was a large
mirror, so hinged and balanced and controlled that
the invalid, lying in the shadowed corner, by a touch
of his hand could alter the angle of the mirror and see

where he wished, taking in all that happened in the world outside. No doubt he was in danger of becoming a gossip, for he knew every detail of life in that village, but at least he was saved from being shut up in the tiny world of his pain. That mirror was his avenue of escape, his window to a wider life, in a real sense his salvation. When God called Job to look on the wonder of creation He was taking him to a window, opening forcibly a way of escape from the world of his own suffering in which he was shut, to his peril. So easily when suffering is very real we can become shut in, asking only : " Why did God have to do this to me ? " We are so apt to think that God is there for our sakes, to minister to our safety and comfort, to make for us the kind of world we want. The truth, of course, is the exact reverse. We are here at all to serve God's purpose, and to do His will. Our own little world is part of a much vaster world in which there is much more at stake than just the happiness, ease and prosperity of me and mine. Sometimes, in our eagerness to shatter the present scheme of things and mould it nearer to the heart's desire we need to be reminded, and very forcibly reminded, of that fundamental fact. The man for whom God does not do what He did for Job may all too easily find only bitterness, or, at best, dull resignation.

Nothing can so release a man from doubt and despair as a greater vision of God. When God answered Job out of the whirlwind He was lifting him out of the idea of God as a petty potentate, taking a fiendish delight in torturing His helpless victims. He spread before His servant the magnificent panorama of the universe and bade him listen to the stars in their courses

> " For ever singing, as they shine,
> ' The Hand that made us is divine '."

He made Job listen, not just to his own bitter, complaining heart, but to a myriad voices crying out

" And shall not the Judge of all the earth, the Creator of the ends of the earth do right ? " He revealed to Job the greatness of the God in whose hand our times always are, and made him content to leave them there.

Two aspects of God's response brought peace to Job's bewildered mind and tortured heart, and always will to men in like circumstances. The first was the reminder, carried to the point of brutal irony, that God knows what He is doing. What a grand picture these poetic chapters give of God holding all within His control ! To the sea with all its relentless power and terror, He " sets bars and doors ", and says : " Hitherto shalt thou come, but no further : and here shall thy proud waves be stayed ". Everything in earth, and sea and sky is harnessed to a great purpose of good. It is a wonderful development of the thought to which the Prologue introduced us, the idea of the Hand on the reins. Freedom, frightening freedom, may be given to sin and death, but never absolute freedom. Through it all God is still in control, and God always knows what He is doing. That was enough for Job, he was content to hold on to that, and it is enough for us, too. That does not mean that all becomes clear, for often, still, we do not understand. It is still hard to understand the degree of freedom God allows us to hurt each other. Some time ago, a young couple returned from the Far East with their two young children under the care of a native nurse. They were living in Northern Ireland. One night in the " small hours " the mother was wakened by a cry. She rushed through to the nursery and found that the native nurse had gone off her head with homesickness and loneliness. With devilish cunning she had drugged the two children to prevent them crying out. She was savagely slashing the face of the older child with a carving knife when the mother burst in upon her. She was found insane and detained " at Her Majesty's pleasure ". The child lived, and was wonderfully patched up. Yet one still cannot understand why God left us with that terrifying kind of freedom, and one can only cling to the assurance that God knows what He is doing. It can never be easy to understand why disease holds such sway, or why death comes as it sometimes does. One does not and cannot understand why so good and fine a man as Eric Liddell, Olympic athlete and courageous Christian missionary, should die of a tumour in the brain. We can only go on believing, often flat in the face of the outward evidence, that God knows what He is doing, that, in a deep and satisfying sense, He does know best, and that even when we cannot understand we still can trust Him.

The other great truth expressed in the peculiar nature of God's response to Job is that while life is fundamentally mysterious, at the heart of the mystery is love. Notice how in these chapters from the Book of Job the mystery of life is not only accepted but emphasized, as if mystery were of the very stuff of life itself. That is abundantly true. The strange fact is that the more we learn the more mysterious life becomes. The scientists may invent marvellous instruments that reach out further and penetrate deeper than ever before, but the mystery grows not less but greater. The old riddle-me-ree remains, the whence-do-we-come, the why-are-we-here, the whither-do-we-go ? But the writer of the Book of Job points us to a Creator who will " cause it to rain on the earth, where no man is ; on the wilderness, wherein there is no man ", who lavishes His specific and generous care upon all His creatures, and can be trusted to care for Man, the crown of His Creation. He makes us more aware than ever of the essential and inescapable mystery of life, but reminds us that at the heart of the mystery is light and not darkness, not cruelty but love. Life *is* mysterious, and we cannot escape its mystery. It is good to take refuge in this, that, in spite of all evidence to the contrary, at the heart of all things stands not grim fate or callous cruelty, but a great love, that amid all the dark clouds and shadowed mystery this remains the abiding truth, " 'Tis only the splendour of light hideth Thee ".

Finally, no experience that brings a man nearer to God can be wholly evil. That is a great final word for Job to speak : " I have heard of thee by the hearing of the ear ; but now mine eye seeth thee ". He has passed from hearsay to a new, more personal and vital experience of God. The rest of the concluding chapter —the Epilogue, which forms the counterpart to the Prologue—describes how complete was the restitution made. The whole story has the happy ending which in every generation alone can satisfy the popular demand. There are born to Job seven more sons and three fine daughters, so that he gets his family back. In material possessions, flocks and herds, he gets twice as much as he had before. All of this may be necessary to ensure that justice is done ere the story ends, but one is left with the curious impression that it is all quite secondary. In a deeper sense Job already has twice as much as he had before, for he has twice as fine an experience of God. There is a knowledge of God to which he has come through his suffering, and by way of despair, that he never had before and could have found in no other way. That does not mean that this happened inevitably, naturally, or more or less automatically, as if suffering were bound, or likely to produce this particular result. Suffering, as we all know now, can too easily degrade and shatter character and faith. As we said at the very start of our study, suffering always tests a man. And how wonderfully most folk stand the test and rise to the occasion !

One specially striking instance of this may, perhaps, be given. It is the story of a man who, during the War, was dismantling a mine when it went off. He wasn't killed, he merely lost both hands and the sight of both eyes. How does a blind man read Braille, and so find release, when he has no fingers ? How does he develop that wonderful extra sense of touch, so often given to the blind, with no hands ? How hopelessly crippled and incurably handicapped that man must be. Not a bit of it ! He became a student in the Department of Commerce in the University of Edinburgh, studying to equip himself for a new job, and to add to his qualifications. But how did he sit exams ? He had an unbiased " reader " who read out the questions to him and to whom he dictated his answers. How was he able to study the subjects he must take, having neither eyes nor fingers with which to read any kind of text-book ? There rallied round him a group of fellow-students who took it in turns to read aloud the text-books to him, while he committed the subject-matter to the almost photographic memory which he developed. All through this period he insisted on leading as normal a life as possible, refusing to regard himself or to be regarded as handicapped and crippled. He took part in all the normal student activities, not excluding dances, and one lady who had actually danced with him remarked that after a bar or two of music she quite forgot that her partner was blind and that the arms, both holding and steering her, ended not in hands but in stumps. Throughout all this there was an atmosphere of happiness and mutual helpfulness about the group of students gathered round this " sufferer " which was most striking. Surely suffering handled in this way is altogether wonderful. Here is a new and rare quality of life which otherwise might not be produced at all.

Ask any minister of wide and deep and varied experience of dealing with human nature who are the people who have made him feel more near to God, and he will unhesitatingly reply that they were, almost without exception, people who had suffered. They were people who had so learned to handle suffering that it brought them nearer to God. More than that, all of them, whatever the nature of their suffering, would bear unanimous witness to this, that they learned

the secret from One whom Job never knew, in whom
God made His Own still more wonderful response than
that given to Job. He spoke this time, not out of the
whirlwind, but with the still, small voice of a newborn
child. He took the problem of suffering, raised it to
the nth power, outlined it against the darkness of
human sin and despair on a Cross to which He was
nailed, and taught us to see there, as nowhere else in
the Universe, that God still knows what He is doing,
even when life seems one hideous muddle of utter
wrong and injustice, and that even when God gives
every evidence of being callously unheeding, or
gratuitously cruel, the wonderful truth is still that God
is Love. During some of the worst trench-fighting of
the 1914 War a young lad amid the mud and squalor
and horror of the trench was brought word that his
brother had been killed. He stumbled down into the
dug-out to be alone with his hurt, took a sheet of
paper, drew on it a rough cross, wrote beneath it
" God is Love " and just sat there, holding on to that
sheet of paper as if there were nothing else to which
he could cling. He was quite right. In face of the
problem as we have tried to study it, or as it came
home so cruelly to him, there is nothing to hold on to
but the Cross and its compelling truth, " God is Love ".

III

THE NOTE OF JOY—FAITH HAILS THE GLORY BEYOND THE SHADOW OF THE CROSS

7

A SOUND PICTURE OF THE PASSION

(a) THE CLINK OF COINS

" Jesus . . . overthrew the tables of the moneychangers."—Matt. xxi. 12.

" He cast down the pieces of silver in the temple."—Matt. xxvii. 5.

IN the early 1940's, just at one of the dark times of the War, there came to many people in Great Britain what was a real spiritual experience, helping their faith to come alive in a new way. It was provided through the broadcasting by the B.B.C. of Dorothy Sayers' Play Sequence *The Man Born to be King*, telling the story of the Life of Jesus both reverently and realistically. Throughout the play very skilful use was made of sound effects, such as the scraping of the bow of a boat on the shingle of the Sea of Galilee, or the drip of water in the basin when Jesus washed the disciples' feet. It was quite astonishing how the story came alive in terms of sound, even to the differing accents of the various disciples, and the varying tones of voice, giving added expression to what was said. Since then many have seen and been helped by a similar series on television, and it is interesting to make comparisons. One's own impression, for what it is worth, is that one was helped more, spiritually, by the sound picture. With television it is dangerously easy to remain a detached spectator ; listening to sound only one felt drawn in. However often and reverently we may remember the events of the last week in the life of our Lord, the remembering will do us little good unless and until we feel drawn in. In this series of studies of the old, old story we shall try to create a sound picture of the Passion. We shall seek to listen to some of the distinctive sounds, for ever associated with the events, and listen for what they may have to say to us. We begin with the clink of coins, a sound of the counting-house and the market-place, which is not religious at all. It is a sound entirely familiar to us, heard in many forms every day. In the story of the Passion we hear it several times, and every one is searching and revealing.

There are the coins that have got out of their proper place. The scene in which we hear the sound of coins for the first time is one of colour and movement in a beautiful setting. It is in the Court of the Gentiles, the outermost courtyard of the Temple on the Dome of the Rock, in the heart of old Jerusalem. It was a truly lovely place with its lofty, gracious colonnades of gleaming marble. It was filled with pilgrims from all round the Mediterranean who had come up for the Feast. They were Jews, most of them, with their strange blend of nationalism and religion, come up to the Temple to worship God, who, they believed, dwelt here in His Temple as nowhere else on earth. Many of them had saved up all their lives for this, and now, at long last they were here in the Courts of God's own House, nearer to Him than ever before. Each had to pay the Temple tax of one half-shekel, and this could be paid only in the proper Temple currency, so they had to change their own money, from the varied currencies of the lands from which they came. The moneychangers, with their tables set out ready, were only too glad to make the exchange, at a percentage out of all proportion to the service rendered. Then the pilgrims would naturally want to make a sacrifice, here in the very sacred heart of their religion. For this they would buy a lamb or other animal which had to be shown to the Temple inspector, to make sure it was without blemish. If the animal had been bought outside the inspector would make a point of finding some blemish so the net result was that the pilgrims must buy inside, and pay the " inside price ". There was a scandalous difference in price, for a dove (the poor man's offering) which cost only four pence outside might cost as much as fifteen shillings inside. The whole area of this outer courtyard was cluttered with the pens of animals, befouled by the dung and the smells, and further complicated, on the occasions of the great Festivals, by the milling crowds. It is difficult for us to realise how this was permitted to go on, but the underlying reason is simple. The common name for all these stalls was " the bazaars of the sons of Annas ". Annas was, of course, the ex-High Priest, and he was behind the whole business, like some huge spider at the heart of an evil web. The whole affair was a huge racket, yet no one could do anything to stop it.

Into this situation comes striding Jesus of Nazareth, with the terrible anger of the strong man who is normally meek and self-controlled. He opens the pens and drives out the animals ; He unfastens the cages, and with a great whirr of wings the doves fly up and away ; He upsets the tables of the exchangers and sends the money spinning in all directions. This is His instinctive and inevitable reaction to such exploitation of man's deep need of God, and He cries out that this place was meant to be a House of Prayer for all nations, and they have turned it into " a thieves' kitchen ". This action of Jesus had two results. He won the ordinary people to Him and for the rest of the week the crowd, with their undoubted sympathy for Him, delayed His arrest. At the same time He signed His own death warrant, for by that action He offended unforgiveably the traders, the priests, and the wealthy Sadducee families. The stand He took meant the end of the only kind of religion they knew, and the end of the money it brought in. They realised, all too plainly, that this was a " show-down " between His way and theirs, that here was an inescapable challenge. It is precisely so for us also ; and we should do well to ask, in the setting of modern civilisation, and not least of " the affluent society ", where we should be listening for that same sound of the neat piles of money being sent violently spinning by Jesus Christ.

Where, in this Christian country, is money getting out of its proper place, where is it leading to the exploitation of human need, and coming between men and God ? There is, for example, the blatant commercialisation of Christmas, which has reached inordinate lengths with Santa Claus in the large stores from the beginning of October, and the whole religious significance of the Festival covered up by the manifold efforts made to " cash in " on the occasion. There is the ever-increasing invasion of Sunday by material considerations ; the deliberate choice of Sunday work because of overtime pay, so that vast numbers of " working-class " folk have no time to attend the church to which they still belong. This is an evil affecting all classes, including the small shop-keeper or tradesman who simply accepts the urge to do the books on Sunday, and the big business man who uses the week-end to entertain potential clients. There is the whole sinister business of certain sections of the press printing what is sordid and smutty, with apparently no desire other than increased circulation. There is the whole subtle, insidious business of vested interests which can cloud the moral issues involved in, for example, the drink trade, and, most recently, the resistance of the great tobacco interests to the Government's campaign against cigarette smoking because of its connection with lung cancer. The same challenging situation exists in connection with world problems.

How much relationships in Africa, for example, are bedevilled by the basic assumption, so long held in varying degrees, that coloured people are merely a pool of cheap labour to be exploited—an attitude often revealed by business people, who complain that the missionaries spoil the natives as labourers. The gravity of this whole problem of the coins that have got out of their proper place is curiously emphasised by the parrot-cry to keep religion out of politics, not to let it interfere with business, never to commit the unforgivable sin of upsetting the apple-cart ! None of us dare forget that one main reason why Jesus was crucified was that He insisted on doing precisely these things and He is still the same. We must still reckon, in our highly complicated society, with this blazing anger of the Lord of all good life. We had better take another look at the pay-packet, the salary cheque, the dividend warrant—yes, even the budget figures of our national expenditure and ask quite honestly where He would send these coins spinning, because they have got out of place.

There is the sound of the coins that told what money can do. These coins give a very tiny almost inaudible sound, yet it is well worth listening for, because they are the two mites given by the widow. Jesus was sitting in the Temple beside the Treasury, which consisted of thirteen trumpet-shaped receptacles into which the worshippers put their offerings, depending on the purpose for which they wished to give. These offerings were, of course, all made in coin, and you could tell the size and weight and worth of the offering by the noise it made. Jesus sitting watching and listening noted something about the way this widow gave her two tiny coins, though they made so insignificant a sound. She seemed to be giving them as an expression of her gratitude, her thanksgiving and her love. Why give both, why not keep one ? With it she could have bought a tiny share of the only meat available to the poorest of the poor, in the market where five sparrows were sold for two farthings. There must have been something in her heart which could only be satisfied by giving all, however little that all might be. Her action and her attitude gladdened the heart of Jesus and helped to restore His faith in that human nature to redeem which He was about to die. Remember, this incident took place on the day of questioning, when His critics and His bitter foes had surrounded Him with their cold and calculating hatred. His reaction to the widow's giving is the same as His wonderful response to Mary's deed when she anointed Him at Bethany.

It is dangerously easy, still, to become calculating, turning everything into terms of cash. A timber-merchant once took his minister with him on a visit to the Borders, on a spring day when the larches were just turning to their peculiar delicate shade of fairy-like green. The minister looking at a whole hill-side remarked how lovely it was, and automatically and instinctively the timber-merchant replied " Yes. That lot should be worth xd. per foot " ! This is surely a very limited attitude, both to life and to the real meaning of money. Money can and should be used as a means to express some of our finer inward feelings. This is true, obviously, of giving at all levels. It applies to the costliness of Mary's gift, making us realise what the gift did and what it expressed. When Zaccheus, confronted by Jesus, said " the half of my goods I give to the poor ", he was using his money to express his contrition for wrong-doing and his joy over his changed life. When Joseph of Arimathea and Nicodemus, both rich men, gave between them a costly tomb and a wealth of spices for the dead Jesus they were using their money to express, however belatedly, what was in their hearts towards Him. That is what money is for ; it is important not for itself, nor for what it can buy, but because of what it can enable us to do and to express. One " pawky " Scots elder used to say " Money isn't everything ; but

it's very handy to go a message with " ! It is indeed—
it is handy to go a message with on the Master's
business ; it is handy to express our concern for the
coming of His Kingdom. The using and giving of our
money is often the only means we have of showing
how much we care for need, known and realised. The
money I give to my church constitutes, whether I
realise it or not, in terms of my total budget, the
measure of my love and gratitude ; it tells how much,
or how little, Christ means to me. At the time of the
Disruption in Scotland when one of the Free Churches
in Ayrshire was opened for worship a servant girl put
£5 in the offering, and her total wage for the year was
£10. That was the measure of her caring. As we
listen carefully for the tiny sound of the widow's
two mites slipping so unobtrusively into the Treasury
let us each ask if we are using our money for
what it was meant to do, and gladdening the heart of
Christ.

Finally, there are the coins that sealed the worst
bargain ever made. We are listening now to the
sound of the thirty pieces of silver. However familiar
the story of the Passion may be the terrible enigma of
Judas haunts the heart every time we read the story.
There are altogether five different accounts of Judas
and his tragic action, but none of them quite satisfy.
Why did he do it ? How could he bring himself to go
through with it ? Was it just avarice, or did thwarted
ambition play its part ? Did he see disaster coming
and decide to cut his losses, and turn King's evidence ?
Even if we accept one or more of these reasons, why
did he settle for so small a sum ? It represented no
more than the replacement value of an ordinary slave.
Judas, after all, was in a very strong position. Caiaphas
and the other leaders were at their wits' end. They
dared not risk a public demonstration in favour of
Jesus, and by Thursday it looked as if they would have
to wait until after the Passover. With two million
people in and around Jerusalem, and all the fiery

feelings which were about, they were sitting on dynamite, and they were quite astute enough to realise it. Judas gave them their chance to arrest Jesus and have Him put away without publicity. Why not stick out for more ? Perhaps the actual sum was only meant to seal the bargain, and commit both Judas and the priests, for all the world like a deposit on the purchase price of a house ! Anyhow, they counted out to him one by one the thirty pieces. Where, one wonders, did he carry them ? Perhaps in the pocket of a leather apron, or in some safe fold of his clothing. Leonardo da Vinci's famous picture of *The Last Supper* shows Judas, three places round the table to the right of the Master, with a bag of money on the table in front of him. But surely not even Judas could have had *that* money actually on the table. That same famous picture, for all its greatness, misses a point when it shows Judas so many places away from Jesus. John's account clearly indicates that Judas was in the place of honour next to the Host, certainly near enough to be handed easily a particular tit-bit from the dish. Judas was clearly told that Jesus knew who the traitor was. It must have been perfectly plain to him that the Master was saving Judas's life by His silence, or by His cryptic words. This was Jesus' last appeal to Judas. Yet Judas resisted it and went out to fulfil his bargain. He hurried through the darkened streets to sell Jesus, to sell the cause for which he had worked for three years, to sell his friend. He went to buy himself out, and to make quite sure that, whatever happened, he was all right. With a crowning ignominy he identified Jesus in the half-light under the olive trees in the Garden of Gethsemane with a kiss, and for good measure kissed Him repeatedly, as if expressing extravagant affection.

How did Judas spend the rest of that night, between Thursday and Good Friday ? Was he, perhaps, alone with Judas, counting out his money, congratulating himself on so cleverly extricating himself from a dangerous situation, gloating over his triumph ? Then in the morning, hovering on the fringes of the crowd, listening to the trial before Pilate, watching the Roman Governor fighting for the life of the Prisoner whom he, Judas, had deliberately betrayed, he suddenly saw what he had done. Then he hurried once again to the Temple, with an even more desperate urgency this time, to give back the money, to go back on his bargain, to undo the whole sorry business. He went to the priests, whose business it was to bring the sin of man, however terrible, to the mercy of God who is infinite in mercy. The priests would have nothing to do with him, told him it was none of their affair, refused in any way to take over from him. So he flung down the coins on the very floor of God's House. We can hear the solid clink of the bag of heavy coins hitting the unresilient marble, then splitting apart and spilling its silver cascade far and wide. Was there ever a more tragic outward expression of what money cannot buy and what money cannot buy back, of all that money cannot do, and all that no money can ever undo ? Then Judas went out and hanged himself. Was it, one wonders, with the thongs of the leather apron that had held the money ? Out of the strange silence when these thirty notorious coins have stilled their clatter we seem to hear a Voice. It asks over the enigma of Judas, " what shall it profit a man, if he shall gain the whole world, and lose his own soul ? " But it does not stop there. For we hear the same Voice praying, from the Cross to which Judas had betrayed Him, praying, surely, even for Judas, unbelievable as it may seem : " Father forgive them, for they know not what they do ". We may never know why Judas did it ; but we do realise that sin is always costly, to everyone concerned ; yet there is One who has " paid the price of sin ". There are no coins in any currency in which we ourselves can pay the price ; but the price *is* paid.

(*b*) THE SOUND OF WEEPING

" When he was come near, he beheld the city, and wept over it."
—Luke xix. 41.

" Weep not for me, but weep for yourselves."—Luke xxiii. 28.

" Peter went out, and wept bitterly."—Luke xxii. 62.

Any visitor who approaches Edinburgh from the south by road will be intrigued by the succession of distant glimpses of the city which follow one another as the road dips and rises again. Finally, he comes over the crest of the rising ground near the Braid Hills and sees the city spreading out before him, with the Castle standing out in the centre. The same was true, with a much greater degree of foreshortening, of the approach to the city of Jerusalem from the region of Bethany. The traveller would keep on catching distant glimpses, and then would, quite suddenly, look right across the deep valley to the city from the slopes of the Mount of Olives. A strange procession is travelling that road ; the focal point of it appears to be a donkey carrying a humble-seeming yet strangely commanding Figure. He is surrounded by a motley, straggling crowd of pilgrims and children, which grows as it moves. It seems to be a glad and triumphant procession, colourful and gay, all bright and happy in the morning sun. As it rounds the bend of the road and the city comes into full view, the procession stops. Evidently there is something wrong. Into the little pool of silence thus created there falls like a stone the sound of weeping. Some hysterical woman, easily moved to joy or sorrow, hardly able to tell where the one ends and the other begins ? Mary Magdalene, perhaps, with her deep emotional nature, finding the occasion too much for her ? No, what we are presented with is the deeply-moving, shocking spectacle of a man weeping, for the source of this incongruous sound of tears is the Figure on the back of the donkey, Jesus Himself. Once before in the story of Jesus, with that intimacy which John uses in the telling, we have been told in the shortest verse in the Bible, " Jesus wept ". On that occasion His weeping was not difficult to understand and appreciate, and indeed honour. He was moved by the heart-broken sorrow of Martha and Mary ; He was sharing deeply in their sense of bereavement ; He was moved—as who could fail to be in such a situation ?—by the " sense of tears in mortal things ". This is different, staggeringly different, and here we must tread reverently and think deeply.

These are the tears of a love that is utterly frustrated and can do no more. It is important to note particularly the exact description given by Luke of what happened. He might have said that the Master shed a random tear, or that for one brief moment a slight moisture dimmed those clear-sighted eyes as they looked on Jerusalem. But no, the word used makes it clear that Jesus broke down completely, and wept uncontrollably. There is something almost indecent, something which makes everyone feel awkward and acutely embarrassed about the spectacle of a strong man, normally holding himself in iron self-control, weeping thus, quite uncontrollably. The only explanation which can be given is that this was truly broken-hearted weeping. It has long been suggested that Jesus on the Cross died of a broken heart, and that the detail which John reports of the spear-thrust into His side letting out blood and water is an indication that this was literally and physically true. This incident on the road into Jerusalem suggests that His heart was broken now, already, before His real agony.

There is a tremendous message here for the world, and for each of us. Here is a revealing measure of His love and caring. You can only weep, thus utterly broken-hearted, for someone or something for which you have really cared very deeply indeed. A scientist may feel sore and disappointed over an experiment that fails. Your big business man may feel disappointed and frustrated over a deal that doesn't come off. Quite soon, however, each of them will just write it off as one of those failures which are part of life. Anyhow, he doesn't break his heart over it, for life in the world of science or business could not go on, on these terms. But Jesus cared passionately for the Holy City, with all its teeming life. He knew every word of the story of its building originally by David, and its very stones, piled generation upon generation, were saturated with the history of His own people. For Him it had a special sacredness. Into it He had been carried as an infant in arms, to be presented in the Temple ; to it He had come as a boy of twelve, at the beginning of His adult life, seeing and marvelling. All of the Jew's deep love of home, his passionate sense of nationhood, was summed up and centred in that great city, towering within its walls, just across the valley. There before Jesus' very eyes was the symbol of what He had come to do ; this was the world in little, a typical representation, in its crowded, narrow streets, its strains and tensions, its strong tides of bitter feeling, of the whole world He had come to save. Here was where He had to begin, in the capital city of God's Chosen People, among His " ain folk ". The bitter realisation comes over Him like a wave, that He has utterly failed with Jerusalem. No wonder He cries " How often I would, and ye would not ". How deeply moving is the homely phrase, drawn from His country childhood in Nazareth, about the hen gathering her chickens under her wings. This has been the passionate yearning of His heart, but His people would have none of it.

Here is the deep tragedy of a love that is given unsparingly and yet is spurned. Here is the final frustration of a love that can do no more. This situation is of the quality of a mine disaster, where the rescue squads have fought against flood water, and fallen rubble and solid rock, taking it in shifts day and night, and now they must admit defeat and accept the fact that it is no longer possible to get any of the entombed men out alive. It is like the tragedy of some terrible fire where a whole wall collapses both on rescuers and those needing to be rescued and the others must stand completely helpless, unable to do anything to save. So it was that day with Jesus ; Jerusalem finally and obstinately refused to listen and He knew that nothing but utter disaster stared them in the face. The city which would not learn the things which belonged unto its own true peace and future security utterly broke His heart.

How is it to-day ? For Jerusalem substitute any other great modern city and how truly we would need to write over it that Jesus beheld the city and wept over it. Could it be Cape Town with its bitter " apartheid " ; or New York with its extremes of wealth and poverty and its hotch-potch of nationalities ; or Paris with its gaiety and glamour and materialism ; or London which proved that it could " take " all the horrors of the Blitz but may not " take " so well the subtler dangers of the " affluent society "—London with the Cross still towering over St. Paul's ; or even Edinburgh, widespread round the great rock that brought it into being, so widely neglecting the challenge of its own motto, " Except the Lord keep the city, the watchman waketh but in vain " ? The weeping of Jesus over Jerusalem is a sound we must not neglect to hear.

The scene changes and it is six days later. Here is another procession, going out of the city in the opposite direction. This is no glad and joyous occasion, this is a procession of defeat. It is led by the Roman soldiers of the execution squad, carrying boards with the accusation against each of the prisoners, then the prisoners themselves, each carrying his cross. It is quite impossible for any of us who have grown up in the modern world to realise the precise nature and quality of the terrific strain to which Jesus had so long been subjected, strain which was not only, not even mainly physical, but on a much deeper level nervous, mental and spiritual. There had been the strain of the Last Supper, with its undercurrents of meaning and feeling, the last appeal to Judas and the bitterness of its failure ; the agony in the Garden ; the crude violence of His arrest ; His succession of trials ; the mockery, the brutality, the horror of a Roman scourging under which a prisoner often died ; the cruel thorns pressed deep into His brow. No wonder we read that again and again He staggered under the weight of His cross from sheer exhaustion. It becomes clear to the centurion in charge that this particular prisoner cannot go on, so the stout shoulder of Simon of Cyrene is pressed into service. When the procession halts for the transfer to be made no doubt there are many to gloat and jeer and cast their taunts. Many are there in the crowd out of lust for blood, which is an ugly and evil thing anywhere and at any time. Then through all the voices there comes the sound of women weeping. Suddenly the lacerated head goes up, the old kingliness returns, and the ring of authority is back in the Prisoner's voice. " Weep not for me, but weep for yourselves, and for your children."

The tears of the women are tears of pity that ought to be changed into heart-searching. This is highly important for our understanding of the attitude of Jesus. All through the story He is concerned mainly not with what they are doing to Him, but with what, in the process, they are doing to themselves. When Judas betrays, what concerns Jesus is what is happening in Judas and to Judas ; what matters about Caiaphas is what he is doing in the name of religion to the only religion Caiaphas understands. All the time Pilate is fighting his losing battle Jesus is troubled over Pilate's hopeless struggle for justice against his own career, and when the soldiers do what they did to Him He is concerned with the effect on them of unquestioning discipline on the one hand and unthinking brutality on the other. When He himself chose to adopt this attitude we must not dare to pity Him. Throughout the story of the last week in His life there is very much that must stir the emotions. If we find in the story nothing to grip the imagination, nothing first to still and then to move the heart, then are we dead indeed to spiritual values. At the same time we must not allow the spiritual effect of our remembering to fade away in merely temporary and superficial emotion. Instead of daring to be sorry for Him, we should ask where and why He might be sorry for us.

It may be true that we have " never had it so good ", but we remain sadly short of true joy and lasting happiness. Our life consists so much in the abundance of the things which we possess, yet we have grasped so little of the unseen realities. We are surrounded by gadgets whose purpose is to make life easier and more comfortable, but we are curiously lacking in true peace and serenity. We have developed to an unprecedented degree the means of getting quickly from A to B, but most of us have pathetically little idea of where we are going in life. On every hand we recognise, if we stop to think at all, that grave problems are coming home to us all, but we have fewer and fewer clear and definite standards of right and wrong and we grow increasingly short of firmly held positive convictions. In the early days of Communism in China a student was tried and condemned to death for propagating this forbidden and dangerous doctrine. As he was being led out of the Court to summary execution he turned to his judges and said quite quietly : " I, at least, know what I'm dying for. Do you know what you are living for ? " Jesus, on the way to the Cross, knew what He was dying for. Tears of pity are out of place. Our thoughts should be turned to heart-searching.

Our third scene is in the outer court-yard of the Palace of the High Priest. It is in the " small hours " of the morning of Good Friday. It is cold, with the bitter cold that penetrates to the very marrow of one's bones, and it is that dead hour of night when vitality is at its lowest. The group of people in the court-yard are just waiting, always a difficult thing to do. The group consists of the Temple guards who arrested Jesus in the Garden and are still on duty, the household servants and Simon Peter. As the time passes we hear his succession of repeated denials of all knowledge of this Jesus, and it is interesting to notice the little detail, that it was his broad Galilean accent which gave him away. Why did he do it ? Peter was essentially a man of action, never happier than when he was doing something, however ill-considered, and perhaps the long inactivity got on his nerves. He was a man of the country-side, at home in the wide open spaces, and perhaps in that situation he felt like a fish out of water. It may be that there is point in the little detail of description that " Peter followed afar off ". He got too far away from Jesus ; again and again in the Gospel story we note how increasingly Peter depended on the nearness of Jesus, and how, on his own, he was always unreliable. It is humanly probable that one denial led to the next. If it is true that " each victory will help you some other to win " it is equally true that each defeat and surrender makes the next one more difficult to resist. Possibly the situation simply got out of hand as each denial plucked at struggling Peter's feet like the undertow of the waves on a shelving beach dragging down a swimmer as he tries frantically to regain his feet.

At that precise moment Jesus is led through the court-yard, and we read " the Lord turned, and looked upon Peter. And Peter remembered ". There is an astonishing degree of deliberation suggested in that phrase " turned and looked ", as if Jesus, consciously and carefully singled out Peter, and by that look separated him from all the rest, until, to all intents and purposes, there was no one there except Peter and the Master he had denied. No wonder Peter " wrapped his face in his cloak " (as an alternative reading suggests) and went out and wept bitterly.

These are tears of self-recognition, that still have

hope and promise in their heart.   If Peter really wrapped his face in his cloak that was an eminently suitable gesture, for by the action of Jesus Peter was not only singled out from the group, Peter was shut in, face to face with himself.   Long ago he had set his feet on the hard road to self-realisation when, on the occasion of the Draught of Fishes he had gone down on his knees in the bottom of his own boat and said to the Master, " Depart from me ; for I am a sinful man, O Lord ".   Now at long last he was really seeing Peter for the first time, the bubble of his self-esteem pricked for ever.   He had boasted of being different from all the rest, and he was different—he was worse than any of the others.   They had only run away, and he had denied his Master, three times.   He was face to face with the grim fact that Peter was the kind of man who could do this awful thing.   Why did Peter not commit suicide ?   He was quite different from Judas.   When Judas, in his turn, came face to face with himself he had nothing left to believe in, or to hold on to.   Peter was different, for he, at least, had that look in the eyes of Jesus to hold on to.   Judas, when he saw with appalling clearness what he had done, tried to undo it, and when he discovered that he was powerless to blot out his failure decided there was nothing left but to end his life.   Peter, on the other hand, realised from the start that what he had done could never be undone, but it was there to learn from.   It is very significant, in view of the important and honoured part played by Peter in the life of the Early Church, that the story of his denial is told quite bluntly in all the Gospels.   It is never glossed over, or toned down, or excused in any way.   Indeed, reading each of the Gospel stories again, one is left with the curious impression that in a strange and wonderful way, as the years passed Peter's denial had become almost something to glory in.   The difference is that Judas was broken utterly, broken beyond repair.   Peter was broken in order to be remade.   In the building of the Forth Road Bridge the engineers used some thirty thousand miles of a special steel wire which is strung across from shore to shore between the two five-hundred-feet-high towers. The strands of wire are laid closely side by side and then compressed into one cable, twenty-one inches in diameter. If for any reason a strand of the wire breaks the two broken ends are inserted into a steel sleeve which is then subjected to great pressure, and the point of the break becomes stronger than the wire itself. In the same way Peter's disastrous failure was to become the point of new-found strength.

Where was Peter after he stumbled out from the court-yard of the Palace of the High Priest ? Somewhere, surely, alone with Peter, like a hurt animal hiding in the dark. Then on Easter Day Jesus found him, how, we do not know, but Paul writing in 1 Cor. xv. and giving our earliest list of the appearances of the Risen Lord definitely stated that He " appeared first to Cephas ". It is difficult but not impossible to picture, with reverence, as we must, that interview between Jesus and Peter. As Peter looked again into those eyes they must have said to him : " Peter, I know exactly what you are, I always have known, and I have told you plainly more than once. Now you know, too. Yet in spite of knowing you as completely as you and I both know you now, I still believe in you, and still trust you." To this Peter must have clung through all those dark hours of bitter tears and agonising self-realisation : " He still believes in me, in spite of everything ". This is the message of hope and promise which must come home to every human heart in the middle of that self-realisation with which the Cross, sooner or later, confronts every one of us. Whenever that same look in the eyes of Jesus singles me out from the crowd, I see what I am and what I have done ; I realise that I, too, have failed him and denied Him ; but I realise, in the self-same moment, that, in spite of everything, He still believes in me and still trusts me. Should not that experience move the strongest of us to tears of wonder and of hope ?

(c) The Drip of Water in a Basin

" Pilate . . . took water, and washed his hands before the multitude."—Matt. xxvii. 24.

He [Jesus] poureth water into a bason, and began to wash the disciples' feet."—John xiii. 5.

The sound of water, in all its varying forms, is a very distinctive sound ; it easily and readily conveys little shades of meaning and with astonishing swiftness and accuracy can conjure up a mental image. It may be the rush of water over a fall in a river, or the chatter and laughter of burn water rippling over small stones ; it may be the sound of water running from a tap or water flowing from a jug or ewer. If one is listening to a radio play, where the sound effects are so important as a means of making the action come alive, and one of the players washes his hands in a basin of water, lifting handfuls of water and letting it fall back into the basin, one can see and sense immediately and precisely what is happening. On two occasions in the story of the events of the last week in the earthly life of Jesus we hear this sound. In the one case it is swift and short, quickly over and done with, with a deliberate air of finality about it. In the other case the sound of water in a basin is repeated twelve times, each time sounding and meaning exactly the same. On both occasions the function of the water is obvious ; it is being used for cleansing, to wash off, or wash away something. There is a kind of common denominator between the two occasions when we hear this distinctive sound, and that is the desire, through the outward act of washing, to get rid of something of which one would want to be rid. The most helpful way of approaching the meaning of these two incidents is not to treat them separately but together, holding both in focus all the time.

We are confronted here by the strange power of Jesus to make us realise our need for cleansing. This He does in the unforgettable action-lesson of the foot-washing in the Upper Room. In view of a misconception of the actual physical situation perpetuated by the great majority of the traditional pictures of the Last Supper it may be helpful to outline what was, almost certainly, the actual position of the characters in this drama. According to the custom of the time the twelve disciples would be not seated but reclining on low couches set at an angle around three sides of a table, much too low for anyone to sit at it in the traditional fashion. With this arrangement they would all be quite near to each other, and each comparatively near to the Master. On this point of comparative nearness questions of precedence inevitably arose. The place of greatest honour was that nearest to the Master, and from this there was a shading off in importance in both directions. It may well be that it was in connection with these " table arrangements " that James and John, the sons of Zebedee, tried to " book " for themselves the two places nearest to the Master, both there and then, and in the coming Kingdom, which they still interpreted in terms of earthly glory. In actual fact, as it worked out, John's very detailed description of the conversations which took place at the table suggests that the place of the most honoured guest, by the deliberate arrangement of the Master Himself, had been given to Judas. At the commencement of the meal there had been undercurrents of conversation, mutterings about the place given to this one or that, and discussions over positions in the coming Kingdom.

There was one omission from the normal procedure, always carried out at such a meal. A servant should have washed the feet of the guests, made hot and dusty by even a short journey through the streets of the ancient city. Among the preparations made with such meticulous care this had not been forgotten, for basin, towel, and water were obviously ready to hand. But for reasons of privacy and secrecy there is no servant present, and where the disciples are all concerned about their own importance and precedence, no one is likely to play the servant's part for the others. It is in this setting that Jesus Himself quite deliberately plays the part of a humble servant. Girding Himself with a towel for an apron He goes to each man in turn, as he lies on one side with his shoulder next the table and his feet away from it. He loosens the sandals from the hot and dusty feet, holds each foot in turn over the basin, pours over it handful after handful of the cool, cleansing water, and then dries the foot with His towel. He begins with John, goes then to Peter, and so on round the table. Surely as the Master did this for each disciple in turn every man saw himself. He saw with terrible clearness his silly pride, his jealousy, his petty squabbling, and was made utterly ashamed. Last of all, if the arrangement of the places was as we have suggested, He would come to Judas. Think how the tension must have built up in Judas's own heart as Jesus went on with the washing, telling the Twelve quite plainly that they were not all clean. Judas must have had a very hard heart indeed to stand up to such a very moving appeal.

Jesus Christ, simply by being what He is, always and inevitably, shows up what others are. The picture galleries of the Vatican are full of immortal pictures by great masters. From time to time you will see a group of art students seated, each with his own easel, around one or other of these truly great pictures, making a copy of greatness with painstaking care. Some of these students already possess real ability, and the pictures they have painted would be of quite striking merit, taken out of that actual situation. It is set over against the work of a true Master that they are shown up as being only second-rate. Take a brand new handkerchief

straight from the box, never used. It looks white,
to all intents and purposes it *is* white. But drop it in
all its fresh whiteness on a patch of virgin snow and it
looks grey. In the same way throughout the story
Jesus, by being there, and by being what He is, shows
up everyone else. We watch the efforts of Caiaphas,
a very astute politician, to bring the first Trial to a
swift and satisfactory conclusion. The calm dignity
of Jesus rebukes his frenzied efforts to secure a conviction. There is a strange parallelism between the
dramatic action of Caiaphas in rending his clothes at
the claim of Jesus, which he triumphantly regards as
blasphemy, and the strange description of the Veil of
the Temple being rent in twain at the moment when
Jesus died. Caiaphas and the kind of religion he stood
for were finished from the moment when he came under
the judgment of Jesus.

The same is true of King Herod, with his cynical
worldliness. He was, we read, " delighted to see
Jesus ", hoping no doubt that this Miracle-worker
would perform some of His " conjuring tricks " for the
amusement of Herod's courtiers. The utter silence of
Jesus before Herod judged him ; even Jesus has
nothing to say to a man like that. The people who
mattered realised that they were being judged. The
disciples all knew it, and so did Pilate. One of the
strangest stories ever written is that of the relationships between the Prisoner and His Roman judge.
There are many indications that Pilate had arranged
late on Thursday night to ratify the verdict at which
the Jewish Court would certainly have arrived, and to
" rubber stamp " the sentence of death. Then he
clearly changed his mind when he held his Court in the
early morning of what was a Jewish Festival. What
made him change his mind ? He saw the Prisoner.
Throughout the conversations and interviews which
followed Pilate was clearly haunted and challenged by
Jesus. Pilate knew men, it was his business to do so.
Out of what he sensed in this strange Carpenter he

fought for the life of Jesus, fought for hours. Repeatedly he declared Him innocent. When at last he was driven to condemn Jesus he simply had to wash his hands. Cynical Roman though he might be, Pilate saw in the light of Jesus the wrongness of what he was doing, his own deep need of cleansing. If you take a basin of water, slightly clouded because it has been used for washing, let the water settle into stillness and look into the water you will see, as in a mirror, your own face. As each disciple looked into the basin of water which Jesus used for the feet-washing, and as Pilate looked on the water with which he had washed his hands of Jesus, each saw himself, and his need for cleansing.

Pilate's kind of washing does not work ; it stands for all time as a symbol of our human inability to be rid of what we have done, and to get back the clean feel once we have lost it. Pilate behaved like the occasional " difficult " sheep at a sheep-dog trial, which twists and turns, doubles back suddenly on its tracks, even attacks the patient sheep-dog, all to avoid being driven through this one gate. Pilate has tried every turn and twist to evade the responsibility of deciding what he alone is to do about Jesus. Now the decision is taken but he still wants to get rid of it. He looks down on the hate-filled faces of the crowd, with their shouts still ringing in his ears. Their native language is not his but he must somehow make them all understand the situation as he sees it. So he falls back on sign language and calling for a basin of water he washes his hands of the whole business, as if to say " I am rid of this Jesus, the responsibility for His death is over to you ". How gleefully the crowd accepted this transfer, crying : " His blood be upon us and upon our children ", and how awful the reality of the fulfilment when in the year 70 the siege of Jerusalem brought death and destruction too horrible to relate. Even so, they did not take the responsibility from Pilate. He may well have thought at that moment : " I wash my hands of Jesus ; I am finished with Him ;

the whole incident is closed ". All over the world in thousands of churches, twice a Sunday when the Creed is repeated, Pilate is still " stuck " with the blame, " Suffered under Pontius Pilate ". There is a memorable scene in Dorothy Sayers' Play Sequence, *The Man born to be King*, when this phrase from the Creed is repeated by differing voices in a host of different languages.

No, Pilate's washing of his hands has not worked. His real need went much deeper than that one unforgettable action. He might get rid of Jesus ; once Jesus was safely dead and there was no going back he might forget Him ; there might be no more left than an odd haunting memory. But Pilate still had to live with himself. What he did that day he did because he could not get away from himself. His behaviour on Good Friday is all in keeping with his known character. He was the kind of man who would use force without feeling. He hated and despised the Jews, yet he could be compelled to back down. He had made mistakes before in handling this touchy nation, and these mistakes had been the subject of complaint. His past caught up with him in his own Judgment Hall, and the day was lost when the voice cried : " If thou let this man go, thou art not Caesar's friend ". None of us can get rid of what we have done, or by our own power change what we have come to be. This basic fact of human experience underlies much of the unrest in modern life. The famous sleepwalking scene from *Macbeth*, especially if played with restraint, can still be deeply moving for a modern audience. This is timeless and unchanging human experience as we know it. That cruelly resolute Queen rubbing her hands to wash off the blood is truly sleep-walking, and that makes the scene all the more telling, this is what is deep down in her sub-conscious mind ; this incurable longing to get back the clean feel is of the stuff of life itself. No one has yet perfected any detergents which can meet this need.

The cleansing Jesus offers does work when nothing else can. Listen again to these two sounds produced in each case by a similar action, the pouring of water from a ewer into a basin. It is very likely that the water in both cases was drawn from the same source, from the new and adequate supply which Pilate had brought into the city, raiding the Temple treasury to pay for it. Why was it that Pilate's use of water would not wash, whereas that of Jesus did and does ? Pilate's hand-washing was an outward gesture intended to put right an inward wrong, and it would not work. Jesus used water as an outward symbol of an inward transaction. This is the significance of His words to Peter when Peter, who could never keep silence how-ever hushed the rest might be, protested : " Thou shalt never wash my feet ". Jesus replied very quietly : " If I wash thee not, thou hast no part with me ", to which Peter responded, with his usual impulsiveness : " Lord, not my feet only, but also my hands and my head ". There are, as most Christians realise, diversi-ties both of belief and practice in relation to the Sacra-ment of Baptism ; some hold that total immersion is an essential of efficacy ; others regard sprinkling as sufficient ; while a few ministers of the " old school " strike a rather unhappy compromise and deluge an unfortunate infant with three good handfuls of water ! Surely it is not the precise amount of the water which is important. It is a sign and seal of an inward trans-action, of a clean start in life, of a covenant " signed and sealed ", of promises made and claimed. It so happens that on the evening of Good Friday, the day when we think again of Pilate's tragic failure, many young people in churches of many denominations, renew the covenant of their own Baptism. This is surely appropriate and significant.

The dark day we now call " Good Friday " offers to every believer that cleansing power which Pilate so pathetically sought, and so tragically could not find. George Bernard Shaw's character Blanco Posnet, the horse-thief making his successful " get-away " from the scene of his latest crime, turns back to get help for a desperately ill child, because there is no one else to go for help in time. Knowing the price he will have to pay in terms of putting his head, literally, in a noose, he delivers his verdict on his own action : " It is worth it to get the clean feel back again ". That clean feel we cannot, by any action of our own, get back again once it is lost. The Cross still holds this great message, which speaks home to this deep need of our nature : " There was no other good enough to pay the price of sin ". If Christ, at such cost has done this for us, and given us back the clean heart, and the right spirit without which there can be no true peace of mind or real happiness for any human being, then here is a great personal challenge. The feet which Christ has washed must not walk again in unworthy ways. The hands that have been cleansed must not again be soiled with wrong. The hearts that have been purified must be kept fit temples for that love divine. We hear again the sound of the water that would not wash, and could not wash the hands of Pilate. We hear the same sound, and with it the voice of Him who, knowing that He came from God and went to God, took a towel and basin—we hear that Voice saying : " Now ye are clean ".

8

AMPLE PROOF OF THE REALITY OF THE RESURRECTION

(An Easter Communion Sermon)

" He . . . gave ample proof that he was alive."—Acts i. 3 (N.E.B.)

THE spoken word, when it is heard by all and sundry, sometimes brings unexpected and not always welcome reactions. Not many people speak back to the preacher in church, however much they may at times feel inclined to do so ! The members of a radio audience do not suffer under any such inhibitions. The immediately preceding three sermons formed part of a series of six addresses under the title " A Sound Picture of the Passion " which, in a much abbreviated form, were broadcast by the B.B.C. in the " Lift up your Hearts " programme on the mornings of Holy Week 1962. They produced, among other reactions, a highly abusive letter from one listener, a self-avowed and militant rationalist, who objected violently to the basic assumptions of the Christian Faith underlying practically every word of this series. " I challenge you to prove ", he protested, " that such a person as Jesus Christ ever existed. There is no verification anywhere in contemporary literature or history of the ridiculous stories which are told only in the Gospels. I challenge you further to prove to the satisfaction of any thinking person this fantastic story that He not only lived and died but rose again from the dead. Dead men do not, in fact, rise from the dead, and you have no right in such a world as this to bid us ' Lift up our hearts ' on the basis of an untruth so obvious and blatant."

Now, this kind of thing is easy to dismiss and many of us may well feel that it is entirely wrong and out

of place even to raise this issue amid the joyful certainty and reverent remembering of an Easter Communion. If anyone does feel like that I would ask
him to consider in this connection two points. Whether
we like it or not this is, in fact, more and more the
attitude of the world in which we live, and very many
people, not excluding a considerable proportion of
those who still go to church, feel the gravest doubts
regarding the reality for which Easter has always
stood. They may sing the triumphant hymns but
deep down in their hearts they do not really believe
the story. The second point is that nothing less than
reality will do, only truth is strong enough to prevail.
In such a world as we are living in to-day you cannot
possibly build a faith for living on a " perhaps ", or a
hoax however ancient, or a lie, however sanctified.
Is there any answer to such a challenge as this ? Can
we give any valid proof that behind this celebration of
Easter Communion is a glorious reality ?

We can point, to begin with, to the fact of the
Church. The mere fact of the existence of the Christian
Church in the world of 1962, if we think about it at
all, must raise most difficult questions. The Church
is a most incredible, bewildering reality, baffling the
understanding, humanly-speaking making nonsense.
We are part of it, one of tens of thousands of such
groups of people gathered on this first of days in the
name of Jesus Christ. We may not normally realise
it but we are part of a very great world-wide fellowship, far bigger than we ever imagine, made up, in the
main, predominantly of weak and fallible folk like
ourselves. Some are, if the truth were admitted,
merely nominal members of any church, our faith and
our " connection " very largely a superstitious survival
from the attitudes of those who went before us and
to whom these things were still real. Many of us are
young, either in years, or in spiritual experience and
have still a lot to learn ; others are older, yet with
increasing years have added little to our knowledge of

the faith, being, in the good Scots phrase, " slow in the uptak ". None of us are as good as we ought to be ; some not nearly as good as we think we are ; yet here we are part, a representative sample of the Church. How shall we picture the Church to-day in its world-wide distribution throughout almost every land, seeking strangely after a new unity, drawn together by a new realisation of one-ness of purpose, driven together by pressure from without, sharing all alike the common dangers of the " Cold War " of unbelief ?

The Church must certainly not, under any circumstances, be compared to survivors of a wreck, huddling together on a raft, or victims of some disastrous flood gathered on an ever-shrinking, tiny island, continually plucked away by the swirling, dark waters. We are more like leaders of a resistance movement met together to plan a final campaign of total liberation. In our own land the most amazing variety of activities are being carried on by the Church ; a fact we must never forget, however perplexed and disheartened we grow at the failure of the Church at local level. The total effort of the Holy Catholic Church throughout all the world is quite tremendous ; the Church of Jesus Christ is directly organising and indirectly inspiring service for suffering mankind as never before. With all its failures the Church is the greatest and most helpful fact of our world to-day. If instead of looking round, honestly and realistically on the contemporary scene, we look back over the generations, we see the Church reaching back into the past and strangely surviving in spite of all weakness from within and every form of pressure from without. How did it happen ?   Where did it begin ?

At the very first Communion Service ever held twelve ordinary men and their Master were the Church in embryo, the tiny seed holding in its frail life the possibility of this incredible growth. When Jesus died on the Cross that Church died with Him. Nothing could be more certain from all we know of that group of men. One of them had betrayed his Master and in so doing had shocked and shaken the others into a depth of horror we can never realise ; the rest had shamefully deserted to save their own skins, and Peter, the only possible leader who could have rallied them again had denied his Master three times and was in the dust of utter despair about himself. Then suddenly, strangely, beyond all reason the Church came alive again in the power of the Risen Christ. There can be no other explanation, either of the beginning or of the continuance of the Church. You cannot possibly build anything so great or so lasting if it is founded on the bog of untruth. The city of Aberdeen in the north-east of Scotland could be quite truthfully described as " the city that came out of a hole in the ground " because so much of that city is built with granite which was hacked out of the enormous excavation of the granite quarry at Rubislaw. In a far truer sense the astonishing edifice which is the Christian Church, the City of God here on earth, came out of a hole in the ground, the rock tomb of Joseph of Arimathea found empty that first Easter day. To me, the fact of the Church is one of the greatest proofs of the reality of the Resurrection, it is impossible to explain the Church if it be not true that " Christ is risen indeed ", that He sustains its life, redeems its errors, forever urges it on and keeps it His.

There is the fact of the New Testament. The New Testament is, pre-eminently, the Book which came out of the experience of the Church gathered around the Risen Lord. The Gospels were written to tell the story, not of the Carpenter of Nazareth but of the King and Head of the Church. The Epistles have been well described as " Letters to Younger Churches ", and they were written, the bulk of them, by a man who was possessed, obsessed almost, by a blazing certainty of the reality, the abiding presence, and the sufficient power of the Risen Christ. The Acts of the

Apostles describes the growth of the Church in those early days and from beginning to end the trumpet note is sounded " This Jesus God raised from the dead ".   In reality the Gospels were all written the wrong way round.   The Evangelists began at the end, started from the strange, incredible dénouement, and worked back to the beginning.   The wonderful beginning which the stories of the Incarnation provide is only the natural complement to the wonderful ending of Easter Day.   If the story had ended on the Cross there would have been no Gospels to write— more, there would have been no gospel to preach. No Easter—no New Testament, it is as stark and simple as that.   And, if no New Testament, then for the great majority of us who are Christians to-day, no Bible.   The New Testament has taken up, fulfilled, and, let us not forget it, carried into circulation the Old Testament.   Together they have provided what is far and away the " best-seller " the world has ever known, with the greatest influence of any single book, translated, in part at least, into well over a thousand different languages to-day.

The Bible is, unquestionably, coming alive in a new way in this generation.   The many new translations have both created a new demand and satisfied a demand, a continuous demand, which already existed. Bible study, in many lands, carried on by the widest variety of ordinary people, has brought home the living, vital message, perhaps as never before. Humanly speaking this does not make sense.   Men still read Homer and Shakespeare, but only comparatively few men and even they not every day ; millions read the Bible every day, and not as one reads the classics, rejoicing in loveliness of language or depth of thought and feeling.   Who, for example, reading the twenty-third Psalm " The Lord is my shepherd ;   I shall not want . . . He restoreth my soul ", ever thinks for a moment that he is reading words originally written two thousand five hundred years ago in a totally different setting ? The Bible is to multitudes a living Word, a Word that speaks straight to the heart of the human situation. The outward form of that situation may change but the central realities abide curiously the same. As H. V. Morton once said, " The pattern of the human heart was patented long ago and the Creator has not so far seen fit to bring out a later model ". The real greatness of the Bible lies not in the fact that it ranks with the great literature of the world—which it certainly does—but rather in the much more important fact that it is the Book that leads us to the Risen Christ and out of which He speaks, still, to the human heart. All our reactions to its every word are coloured by the light of the meaning He gave to it. It is from the pages of this Book that all over the world to-day, in every kind of Christian Church, worshippers have listened at Communion to the words of the " warrant " or the institution of this Sacrament, words which in their essence sound almost like directions for the production of a drama—" This do, in remembrance of me ". In that same way this wonderful Book of the Risen Christ reaches out to all sorts of situations, telling us what we are to do, instructing us how to handle life, touching life at many points, and, like the Master Himself, transforming everything it touches.

It is strange in what unlikely places and seemingly unsuitable situations this power of the Word to speak naturally and directly can be demonstrated. The members of the Scottish Rugby XV together with the officials of the party were driving through the dark streets of Dublin in the " wee, small hours " of the morning on the way to the Airport after the thrills and triumphs of a victory over Ireland, tired but happy, no doubt. Someone started to sing " The Lord's my shepherd " to the tune Crimond. In a moment that entire bus-load of men had taken up the tune and were singing it, in full part-harmony and word perfect right through to the end. I somehow think David himself would have appreciated it ! When the United States Atomic Submarine " Skate " was carrying out her perilous voyage of survey beneath the ice of the North Pole she surfaced one day, which happened to be a Sunday, in one of the " lagoons " of thinner ice amid that chilly vastness. The Commander thought he would hold a Church Service but the solid ice began to close in and they had to submerge suddenly. They carried out their Service just the same, deep below the Arctic ice, and the Commander read from Psalm 139, " Whither shall I go from thy spirit ? or whither shall I flee from thy presence ? If I ascend up into heaven, thou art there : if I make my bed in hell, behold, thou art there. If I take the wings of the morning, and dwell in the uttermost parts of the sea ; even there shall thy hand lead me, and thy right hand shall hold me." A patient in hospital, rushed there in an emergency, adapting herself as best she could to this strange new world, found by her bedside a little framed text containing words which, because of the most famous hymn, probably, in the English language, are utterly familiar : " Abide with us ; for it is toward evening, and the day is far spent ". As she looked and faced her own personal situation, the meaning of the words suddenly shone out as never before and through them she discovered the reality of the presence and the power of the Risen Christ. But " if Christ be not risen " then these words would never have been written. No one in Dublin could have said " The Lord *is* my shepherd " ; no company of men under Arctic ice could have believed " thy right hand shall hold me " ; no woman, even in her greatest need could have been assured of a reality so unlikely. The New Testament itself is ample proof that Christ is alive.

Finally, and by far most cogent, there is the fact of personal experience. Much of the heat and argument engendered in an issue of this kind arises from our failure to recognise that there are different kinds of proof, relevant in varying situations. There do exist—and we must just face it—situations in which a questioner simply cannot be given the kind of proof he demands, simply because, in that setting his demand is really *ultra vires*. The listener who wrote challenging me to prove that Christ ever lived, or died, or rose again signed himself " Invictus " and the attitude he expressed was one of not only invincible but vindictive, cynical, snarling unbelief with which one can do nothing. There are people who take a stand of this kind, for one reason or another, and there is no common ground on which we, who hold the Christian faith, can meet them. In a sense, this kind of article of our faith is one you cannot " prove " to anyone else. The best you can do is to remove doubt, or to buttress faith which is already there. But the only truly satisfactory proof is to be found in the unshakable reality of personal experience. This seems to me as a minister dealing with people in all sorts of situations of joy and sorrow, watching them handle life decisively and successfully, or crack and go to pieces under its varying pressures and tensions, to be precisely the quality of proof for which real people are looking. What will really satisfy our minds which search for truth and our hearts which hunger after reality is not logical demonstration which could convince a coldly-detached investigator. What we are all seeking after is some practical demonstration made available in terms of human lives like our own, and subject to the same strains and stresses that " Christ's touch has still its ancient power ", and that He still does for actual people to-day exactly what He did for Peter and Andrew and Matthew and Mary Magdalene and the others in the days of His flesh.

It is when I come across a man or woman, not necessarily very outstanding in any of the ways in which we customarily measure ability or success, taking hold of life and using it wisely and well, winning from it real happiness and satisfaction, often in simple ways, holding it in reverent hands, gratefully, as a trust from God ; or facing with courage and fortitude " the slings and arrows of outrageous fortune ", accepting disappointment, or the defeat of cherished plans, or pain and suffering as something in whose heart the love of God is still at work—when I see these things and know that the secret is plain and unmistakable—here is a man or woman in whose life the Risen Christ is a vital, ever-present reality, then I know I am being given " ample proof that He is alive ". This element in life, the faith of ordinary people that Christ still stands among us in His risen power seems to me to provide one of the finest proofs of the reality which underlies this Easter Day. But, of course, in itself even this is not enough.

We are here to-day to get a new grip of the full wonder which this Easter Day sets before us. We are here at the Table of our Lord to hear Him say, not just to all, but to each : " Take, eat. This is my body which is broken for you." We are here to lay hold with real eagerness on that certainty of conviction which in such a bewildering world continually eludes us. There may be some of us who will hold these symbols in the cupped hands of one who is really suffering and carry the chalice to lips that tremble with eagerness. If we can do that, then the critics are answered as far as we, at least, are concerned. I have found here again on this Easter Day a personal certainty which nothing must ever shake. I am one of the men and women, to whom in all generations He showed Himself after His death, and gave ample proof that He was alive.

9

THE RISEN CHRIST—THE HOPE OF GLORY

" How are the dead raised up ? and with what body do they come ? "—1 Cor. xv. 35.

THIS is unquestionably one of the greatest chapters in the whole Bible, a chapter which deals honestly and courageously with the one inescapable fact in life, which is the fact of death. " What will happen to me when I die ? What has happened to those whom I have loved and lost a while ? " These are questions which can never entirely and permanently fade from our minds and hearts, even if to dwell on them is morbid. Every now and then, often quite without warning, this fact of death leaps out from ambush, as it were, and confronts us. There is no evading it ; there is no means known to man of ignoring its existence and getting away with that pretence. In this chapter Paul faces it, fairly and squarely, and lays down a great principle, which he states with ringing conviction. He reminds us what is at stake here, making it cruelly plain that " if Christ be not risen " then there is no real content to our faith, for the word " vain " means literally " there is nothing in it ". In the famous Hawes Inn at the south end of the Forth Bridge there are photographs preserved of the various stages of the building of what is one of the famous bridges of the world, some eighty years ago. One of these photographs shows the central pier of the bridge towering up from the firm foundation of the tiny rocky islet of Inchgarvie in the centre of the estuary, and from that main tower the archways being built out in either direction. In the same way Paul builds up and out from his central, rock-like conviction of the resurrection of Jesus Christ, fashioning a faith which reaches out on the one hand towards God in a new glory of faith in His power and love, and on the other into a great new conception of our human life and destiny.

This is a good time, in the afterglow of Easter itself, to study what this chapter teaches; to look at this fact of death, and all its effect upon our human lives, in the light of our thinking of the Resurrection appearances of Jesus Christ under the guidance of Paul's teaching in this chapter. We are very apt to surrender the attempt to think honestly about death, almost before we have begun, simply because we can never get away from this grim realisation, which we may seldom express, but which continually bedevils our thinking : " No one has ever come back from the other side of death ; we are just guessing and groping ". Paul's blunt answer to this is quite uncompromising : " You are wrong. Christ came back, and there is much we can learn about our own destiny from the nature of His life, once He had passed through death ". Now, we must not assume too much. It may well be that the ringing statement of the familiar Easter hymn " Made like Him, like Him we rise " is not the central meaning of the Resurrection, but only a derived consequence. At the same time it can be most instructive for us to think in terms of His risen body as we seek to understand what it is we mean, and what we do not mean when we express our faith in " the resurrection of the body ".

As we look at the stories of the Resurrection appearances of Christ and put them together we are reminded, very forcibly, how He has transformed completely all our thinking about these bodies of ours. We must be careful not to isolate the Resurrection but to put it in its rightful setting in the total picture of all Christ has done to change our idea of the human body. The story of the life of Christ, as we remember on Easter Day, was written the wrong way round, and the beginning was seen in the light of the end. From the end we must go back to the beginning, taking in, in the process, all that lies between. We have to go back to the Incarnation, the coming into flesh, the becoming flesh and blood. The whole emphasis of the stories of the Incarnation, whether factually described, as by Luke, or philosophically interpreted, as by John, is laid upon the fact that in Jesus God became really and truly human, bone of our bone, and flesh of our flesh ; He grew by all the normal processes of growth ; He learned by trial and error, as we all do, that precise co-ordination of heart and mind and hand, which can make human personality so finely adapted to express character and fulfil the purpose of God. Jesus had a body which, it is expressly stated, grew tired, hungry and thirsty, could and did both laugh and weep, longed, with every fibre of its being for peace and rest. His was real flesh, which could be torn cruelly by scourging, and lacerated by thorns, and from which the blood could ebb away. Yet all the time this was God Incarnate, God in a human body.

All this is saying, not least to this generation, something tremendously challenging. The body, we are told, is a clog, a prison, a handicap, the lower part of me, dragging down my higher self. This has been accepted teaching and preaching for many centuries, and the body has been decried as " this muddy vesture of decay ". We now have a not dissimilar teaching in modernised form, telling us, with all the modern jargon, how it is ruled (so that it rules us) by glands, hormones, instincts, desires and passions. It is high time we recovered the belief which flames through the New Testament that the body is something God has lifted up and transformed, God has given to it, in Christ, a new dignity and sacredness. In the busy town of Penrith, on the fringe of the Lake District, there is an old Inn which proudly displays a sign stating that " Prince Charles Edward Stewart slept here ". So, an Inn acquires a new dignity, a new worth, an abiding attraction two hundred years later, simply because a Prince spent a night in it.   How much more important to say again of this human body : " A Prince lived in this for fully thirty years ; there has been more of God revealed in a human personality, body, mind and spirit than in anything else in the whole creation ".

There is a little poem which says this finely, the poem *This Quiet Dust* by John Hall Wheelock,

> " Here in my curving hands I cup
> This quiet dust—I lift them up.
> Here is the mother of all thought,
> Of this the shining heavens are wrought,
> The laughing lips, the feet that rove,
> The face, the body that you love :
> Mere dust, no more—yet nothing less ;
> And this has suffered consciousness,
> Passion and terror ; this again
> Shall suffer passion, death and pain
> For, as all flesh must die, so all,
> Now dust, shall live.   'Tis natural ;
> Yet hardly do I understand—
> Here in the hollow of my hand
> A bit of God himself I keep,
> Between two vigils fallen asleep."

This is a way of thinking about the body which has great consequences.   It is high time it was applied, for example, to our thinking about Christian marriage. We badly need to rediscover, in this connection, the sheer sacredness of personality and to recall that Christian marriage means the blending of two whole lives into one new unity, not merely the legitimising of the purely physical union of two people.   But this goes further, for this way of thinking takes the physical side of marriage and deliberately lays on it the sacredness of God.   The two shall become one flesh—this is the holy ordinance of God.   The phrase from the traditional Marriage Service " with my body I thee worship " means precisely what it says, and to say this as part of a Christian Service is not at all indelicate ;

N.U.S.—8

it is only claiming this sacredness of all life. Here, too, is a refutation of the idea that God is only concerned with our higher life. Jesus was always concerned with the whole personality. It is falling tragically short of the full Christian position to say or suggest that Christ is concerned with saving our immortal souls, that He is interested in the way we say our prayers, but He is not concerned or interested about the way we earn our wages or the fact that so many of " God's children " are hungry or homeless or riddled with disease. Communism is guilty of the heresy of reducing a man to no more than a mouth to feed, and hands to harness to the tasks of the State. We can be guilty, all too easily, of the opposite error, that of assuming that he is only the " soul " somehow to be saved in strange and artificial isolation from his body.

The final great consequence, however, is that the whole of life is sacred. What Paul is saying in this chapter is, in effect, " God, who in wisdom and power has given you this wonderful body in this life, will give you another when this body dies. Christ has come to save and renew the whole of you." As Christians we do not believe in the immortality of the soul, we believe in the resurrection of the body. This is where the stories of the Risen Christ can make complete our thinking and believing about the body. We read in these stories on more than one occasion that His disciples thought that He was a disembodied spirit. He was at pains to disabuse them of this error, convincing them that this is precisely what He was not. The body of the Risen Christ challenges us to rethink our ideas of life after death and to find room for three reassuring principles.

There is the principle of continuity. Christ's Resurrection body was the same, recognisably the same, and yet different. His body now existed under utterly different conditions. We must stress that in order to remove and counteract an entirely super-

stitious idea which has persisted far too long. This
is the idea that when we say " I believe in the resurrection of the body " we mean that the actual physical
body which, as we all know, has mouldered in the
grave, will magically be reconstituted. Without undue
unkindness to those who hold such a belief in all
sincerity it must be said that this is tragically short of
our true Christian faith. On 21st May 1650 the Marquis
of Montrose was publicly executed for treason at the
Mercat Cross of Edinburgh. His body was then dis-
membered ; the trunk was buried beside the public
gallows on the Boroughmuir ; the head was fixed on
a spike on the Tolbooth ; the arms and legs were
sent to be displayed at Stirling, Glasgow, Perth, and
Aberdeen. At the Restoration the Scottish Parliament
resolved that his scattered members be gathered
together and " interred with all honour imaginable ".
This was done in 1661 and the head, the trunk, and
one arm were buried in St. Giles'. In 1930 Dr. Warr,
minister of St. Giles', was offered an arm, purporting
to be that of the Duke of Montrose, preserved by a
devout Jacobite family. Because its authenticity
could not be absolutely established the arm was not
buried in St. Giles' but preserved at the family seat of
the Duke of Montrose at Drymen. The extreme form
of the literalistic belief in " the resurrection of the
body " is that in the Resurrection Day this arm will
come from Drymen, and be joined by the missing legs,
wherever they may be, and reunited with the rest in
St. Giles'.

In this very chapter Paul states, as categorically as
possible, " flesh and blood cannot inherit the kingdom
of God ". " This corruptible " is a true and factual
description of our purely physical and material being,
and it must, obviously, put on incorruption. Even a
moment's serious and honest thought would make it
clear that nothing less will do. On a visit to Italy
shortly after World War II, I went to Assisi, because
of its associations with St. Francis. An unexpected

" extra " was a visit to the tomb of Santa Chiara, St. Clare. Her embalmed body lay there under glass, for all the world like the Crown Jewels, almost exactly as she was when she died six hundred years ago. I have never seen anything so dead in my life, never looked on quite such a travesty of life. We have only to think of the crippled or decayed travesty of a healthy body with which some people die to be ready to pray, fervently : " God forbid that we should ever be given back the body in which we die ".

Yet continuity there is, and must be. The body of the Risen Christ is so different that His best friends do not at first recognise Him, yet He insists and proves that He is the same Jesus. John wrote what is generally regarded as the most " spiritual " of the Gospels. Yet it is he who begins by declaring that " the Word was made flesh " and who, near the end, tells the story of the Risen Christ with His " spiritual " body, offering Thomas the proof of His hands and His side. There was always something by which He could be known and recognised, the tone of His voice, or the familiar gesture with which He broke the bread. He and His own still, without hesitation, called each other by name. Amid all the mystery let us cling to that. It has been finely said : " Those who love God never meet for the last time ". We shall still be recognisably ourselves. This truth carries both challenge and comfort. You *can* take it with you, whatever you have achieved in the way of being the best that you can be ; not money or fame, but just the self you have fashioned by the grace of God. We shall know and be known ; we shall take up life together where we left off.

The second principle is that of contact, and more than contact. In spite of all the bitter and unmistakable separation of death we can still be in touch. It is a significant feature of the appearances of the Risen Christ that He so often offered them direct contact with Himself ; they sought to touch Him of their own accord, or He invited them to do so. Once that contact was established He led them on, gently but firmly, beyond the need of such outward contact. It is highly important that the Risen Christ never merely " appears ". He always came to do something for them, and the first thing He did was to bridge this gulf of death. This is still our primary and painful need. The bitterness of death is first felt when we realise the awful blank gap that is left, contact is completely broken, we are out of touch. There is no more service our love can render to the one who is gone from us. In this connection it can bring much-needed healing to recognise, as soon as possible after the original parting, that there is something left to do, an unfinished task to be carried on, an interest shared in life to be kept alive. There can be few stories from real life which reveal such utter desolation of grief as that of Marie Curie when her husband, Pierre, was so tragically and wastefully killed in an accident. Being an agnostic she did not have the consolation of the Christian faith, and she had to find what healing she could in flinging herself sacrificially into the continuance of the tasks which he and she had shared. How much more than this we can enjoy, if we will but claim the glory of our inheritance. From our human side we can, indeed, go on working at the tasks they have left unfinished, and still savouring the joys we once shared with them, though now these may be bitter-sweet. But there is a wonderful other side. We think and speak of the other life as a life of service. What may that service be ? They may be " like the angels ", but what do angels do ? How do they serve God ? We believe that this other life and our own are strangely and wonderfully interrelated. Would it not be just like God to use our own as His messengers to us from the other side ? Professor A. J. Gossip once said that there are things which happen which " feel like the touch of familiar hands ". As a beautiful hymn expresses it :

" O fuller, sweeter is that life,
    And larger, ampler is the air :
Eye cannot see nor heart conceive
    The glory there ;

Nor know to what high purpose Thou
    Dost yet employ their ripened powers,
Nor how at Thy behest they touch
    This life of ours."

Finally there is communication. In the stories of the Resurrection appearances a very interesting fact emerges, one whose significance dawned only slowly on the followers of Jesus. Even when they did not think He was there, He still knew what they were saying and even thinking. This emerges clearly in the story of Thomas, for Jesus quotes almost verbatim what Thomas has said, although He was not then visibly present. Gradually these men and women come to realise that they can speak to Him at any time, and turn to Him anywhere. There is communication, and the traditional expression of that, although its meaning is dulled by over-familiarity, is the Communion of Saints. This doctrine meets a deep-felt longing of every human heart. It is this longing which the Spiritualist seeks to satisfy through a human medium. Yet, God be praised, we need no such medium. Very often someone facing the readjustment which follows bereavement will say to me : " I find myself turning to X as if he were still there, to say something to him or share some experience with him, and I have to draw myself up ". If you feel like that then say it ! Keep open the lines of communication. Truly rejoice in the Communion of Saints.

At the same time we must be prepared to be challenged by the reverse side of this thought. If they know, all the time, what we say and do, then how must they feel at times ? How often, in terms of the old Scots song, we " grudge them sair tae the land o' the leal " ! How they must be hurt by our careless forgetting, or, at other times, by our broken-hearted refusal to take up the life that is left. Surely the worst possible betrayal of the trust they have left, and still share with us, is to allow all life to tumble in, a pile of ruins, of mourning that leads to self-pity. How much better, and more truly Christian, to take up life and go on, with their eyes, now seeing so much more clearly, upon us at every stage, living for the time when we shall meet again. How wonderful then to discover that there is no gap to be bridged, and no strangeness to be overcome, for we have been in constant fellowship and unbroken contact from first to last.

10

WHITSUNDAY—THE BIRTHDAY OF THE CHURCH

" Do you not know that your body is a shrine of the indwelling Holy Spirit, and the Spirit is God's gift to you?"—1 Cor. vi. 19 (N.E.B.).

THIS day, Whitsunday, is the real birthday of the Christian Church. Although Easter Day, with its glory, had come and gone, the followers of Jesus were still in a state of waiting and preparation ; the Church had not yet really been born. In a sense the " Christians " were doing nothing, yet they were eagerly looking forward, on tiptoe of expectation. The situation and atmosphere were almost exactly those of the days immediately preceding D-Day. Then came the tremendous experience of Pentecost ; the Church began, and the end is not yet in sight ; something was started that nothing has been able to stop. There came alive a new reality in the world, a reality which men, try as they may, cannot kill or destroy, either by persecution from without or apathy from within. All this happened in virtue of a great gift. That day it was as if a good fairy touched the life of the infant Church and gave the endowment of the gift of the Spirit. How often the good fairy bringing gifts has truly been present in real life at the birth of a child ! Wolfgang Mozart, Yehudi Menuhin, Kathleen Ferrier, Thomas Edison, Frederick Banting, Alexander Fleming—surely the good fairy was present at the moment of the birth of each to impart a great gift. In every one of these cases the original gift had to be cherished, developed, brought to its fulfilment. Yet none of the great achievements with which these names are connected would have been possible without the initial endowment.

Precisely the same thought is in Paul's mind when he declares " the Spirit is God's gift to you ". Here is the initial endowment given to every Christian, and it is this which makes the Church possible. There is perhaps no doctrine which we find more difficult and about which it is so dangerously easy to be vague and muddled. In simplest terms, the Spirit is the gift of God Himself, whose nature it is to give. God gave Himself in the act of creation, supremely in the marvel of the life He has made in His own image ; He gave Himself for our redemption in Christ ; on Whitsunday He reached a further stage of self-giving, giving Himself to dwell in us. This gift is given to each and every one of us ; the gift is no longer reserved for the few and for rare persons, granted only for some special purpose. In the New Testament from this point we find the phrases " the Spirit of God ", " the Spirit of Christ ", and " the Holy Spirit " almost as if they were completely interchangeable, yet all are of God. The great story of Pentecost has two sides to it ; the gift came to all of them together, and the " togetherness " seems to have been a condition of the gift, but it became divided up, distributed, dealt out, almost, until it became the individual, personal possession of each. There is nothing the Church needs more badly than to renew, reclaim and recover this original endowment of the Spirit. Such a recovery can do for each of us three things which seem nowadays to be more important than ever.

The gift of the Spirit gives a new sense of sacredness to life, and to the whole of it. In this text Paul begins with a picture which he uses more than once, the picture of a shrine. In Edinburgh one thinks inevitably of the centre Shrine of the War Memorial on the Castle Rock, a truly and obviously sacred place. For anyone to defile it is quite unthinkable, no one in his right mind could do that. The same is true of any sanctuary, whether it be a great church like St. Cuthbert's Church here in Edinburgh, with its marble Communion Table and the alabaster mural of the Last Supper, or some tiny chapel, or some plain and simple country kirk, the place has a quality of sacredness. If anyone were to mutilate the face of Christ in such a mural, or put up some obscene picture in front of any Communion Table we should react with a sense of instinctive horror at the degradation and desecration involved. This is the thought of our own human personality to which Paul is directing us. Our age has seen a wide and literal " de-secration " of human life. Our human personality has largely lost its dignity, its worth and its sacredness. We have suffered twice within living memory the horror and bestiality of total warfare ; we have undergone the subtle, subversive de-personalising influences of the machine age ; now we all live under the threat of nuclear destruction, so much worse than Nature, so much more " careless of the single life ". Our human life is treated as if it were some cheap and shoddy prefabrication, not a shrine. We are becoming cheap to ourselves and making ourselves cheap. Our scales of values have become completely overturned so that, in very many aspects of life, that which is essentially shoddy, tinsely and cheap is over-valued.

One of the less fortunate by-products of the " affluent society ", especially in Great Britain with its Welfare State, is that the main ideals for life are to be safe and comfortable, and our life, in aiming at and largely achieving these ideals, has become devoid of dignity, worth and abiding values. It is a tragic feature of our life to-day that crimes against the person are on the increase, and one hears, far too often, of some old person cruelly beaten up for the little she may have in her purse, or the few shillings he may have in the till. At the same time there are much more subtle crimes against personality, in a world where we are subjected to so many influences that, quite literally, degrade human personality, and drag it down to the lowest level. In this setting it is high time we listened again to Paul reminding us : " Your body is a shrine ". We can apply this in the context of sex and its many abuses, both in thought and practice. In Christian belief " I " am not just a soul, which can mean something comfortably vague ; I am also a mind and I must think of what I take into my mind, what I read, what I watch, that on which I focus my thinking, what I permit to float upon the screen of my imagination. This much is obvious, but we must go further. In a recent ecumenical conference on Christian Stewardship the Greek Orthodox Church rather startled the rest of the delegates by its blunt and unashamed emphasis on stewardship of the body, as a shrine to be kept white and whole, every bit as much as is the sanctuary of the soul. We badly need to recover this sense of the sacredness of the body, as something which cannot be unclean in itself for God made it. This is needing to be said not least among the more irresponsible of our teenagers, but still more in " intellectual " circles. In a discussion on Christian morality a minister whose work lies mainly among University students protested, with much feeling, about the suggestive kind of stuff they have been taught and accept as " gospel " in terms of the great " god " psychology, that the body is a delicate instrument full of impulses and urges which it is wrong and dangerous to control or direct. Yes, it is high time to re-state this positive idea : " Your body is a shrine of the indwelling Holy Spirit ", and to recover our belief in the Holy Spirit as being, in the deepest sense of the word, our Sanctifier.

The gift of the Spirit imparts a new sense of being both used and useful. Here is a wonderful extension of an idea which was previously strictly limited in its scope. In Old Testament times it was generally recognised that rare people were peculiarly used by God for special purposes. Moses, Samuel, and the prophets—they all fitted into His plan, and were peculiarly equipped to play their parts therein ; it was all right for them, but we are left out. Pentecost, in a very special sense, is the Christian Charter of the common man, because it both declared in theory and operated in practice that ordinary people, without exception made for any reason, are all being used by God. The glorious significance of Whitsunday is that it stands essentially for God in me, working through me, using my hands, my brain, my strength, my skill to get done what He wants done in His world. This is the truly great idea which in our day has become almost a lost idea. Many of us in recent days have been learning to think, perhaps for the first time, in terms of Christian Stewardship. It is very tempting to think, at least at first, of a rather limited conception of our Stewardship, to reckon up the time we spend in what is directly church work, the talents we dedicate within the life of the Church itself, the material possessions we offer in its service. To think along these lines is undoubtedly a help, and leads generally to better service, more worthy giving, and new vitality all round, but it is not enough. What about applying the principles of Christian Stewardship where I am from day to day, in the job I do for a living, in the business of earning my daily bread ? What about my Stewardship there ? Is it possible to think, in that down-to-earth setting, of God in me, getting done through me what He wants ?

If we are honest we must admit that in many cases this is very hard to see. It is much easier to picture myself as one tiny cog, very unimportant, in the vast, complicated machine of production and distribution. There can be little doubt that our whole attitude to daily life and daily tasks would be transformed overnight if we could learn again to know that, even there— yes, there more than anywhere—we are both being used and being useful. Dr. William Barclay's *More Prayers for the Plain Man* expresses this principle most suggestively. He has, for example, " Prayers for a Teacher, a Doctor ; for those who serve the Community in Town Councils, Trade Unions, and Public Service ; for Shop Assistants, for Office-workers, for Nurses, for Policemen, for Civil Servants ". All these types of people and hosts more would be helped by making a day-to-day rediscovery that God can and does use ordinary people in everyday situations. This would make, for one thing, all the difference to our readiness to respond to the prompting of the Spirit. From time to time we are privileged to see, amid the strange intermeshing of one life with others, among all the threads of connection which seem to cross at random, how God actually gets results, how His goodness and mercy do in fact work out. We should not be surprised at this. When a man in a capsule whirling through outer space can be kept under remote control and in constant communication, why should we be surprised that God the Father speaks to us through His Spirit dwelling in us, and directs us, if we are willing to listen ? A year or two ago a minister in Edinburgh going about his ordinary visiting was suddenly seized by an overwhelming urge to visit a particular elderly woman member. There was no ostensible reason why he should go, but the impulse was as clear and definite as if a voice had actually spoken in his ear : " Go at once and see Mrs. X ". Under this impulse which was not to be disobeyed he went to her house, got no answer to his ring, eventually forced an entry and found her lying unconscious in a gas-filled room, having turned on the gas-ring under the kettle without lighting it properly. Was this chance, coincidence, telepathy, or a clear and dramatic instance of God, through His Spirit, directing one of His servants, and using him to fulfil His purpose of saving a life ? No one is left out, none are useless. There is never anyone to whom God, caring for the whole world and for the individual life with such infinite compassion, will ever say, kindly but firmly : " I am sorry, but I have no use for your services. There is no way in which I can use you, there is no opening for the likes of you."

The gift of the Spirit gives to the life of each and every one of us a new sense of extra resources When, on the birthday of the Church, this priceless gift of the Spirit was given, every life to which the gift was shared out and in which the Spirit was appropriated, found an extra endowment, developed a new quality. When we read the chapters of the Book of the Acts which follow the story of Pentecost we gain, ever increasingly, the impression of quite ordinary people who had come to live in a new dimension, with totally new possibilities at every level of their personality, physical, mental, moral, spiritual. The disciples before and after Whitsunday are as different as handicapped patients before and after one of the modern miracles of surgery. It is as if, previously, they had always been handicapped in every aspect of their being, and now they were liberated into a completely new kind of life. They are bolder and braver, they can face hardships with a new endurance, they can tackle problems and solve them in the power of an added intellectual endowment ; they live and move and have their being against the background of pagan practice and superstition with a rare moral quality which stands out like a lily on a dunghill ; most important of all, they are increased out of recognition in spiritual stature, in the Scots phrase they are " further ben " than one, knowing them from the Gospels, would ever have believed to be possible. It is the indwelling power of the Spirit which has provided this quite marvellous extra and made all this possible at all.

To " find an extra " is the great demand of our own day. We need this, obviously, merely to muster up sufficient resources to be equal to the demands, the normal demands of ordinary, everyday life. It was stated recently that in Great Britain to-day one bed in every three in all our Hospitals is occupied by a patient suffering from mental or nervous trouble. The reason generally given, as a kind of G.C.M. of all the personal variations, is that we are not able, under modern conditions to handle life decisively ; for one reason or another, real or imaginary, it gets on top of us. By comparison with the years of economic stringency and real hardships, by comparison, most immediately with the bitter years of war, it seems that we could stand danger, and even face disaster with astonishing equanimity and resiliency, but we cannot stand prosperity. This is true of all of us, and we do well to remember that the Church is made up of ordinary people ; it is not so much a haven for saints, as a hospital for sinners ; we are subject to precisely the same strains and stresses as all other fellow-men and women, but we have, or we should have, an extra to enable us to stand these strains and face these stresses. That extra is the Spirit dwelling in us, to strengthen us when we are weak, to steady us when we are like to fall, to guide us into truth when we do not at all know what to believe.

In the words of a hymn we sometimes sing without truly accepting its meaning :

" Teach me to feel that Thou art always nigh ;
   Teach me the struggles of the soul to bear,
 To check the rising doubt, the rebel sigh ;
   Teach me the patience of unanswered prayer.

Teach me to love Thee as Thine angels love,
   One holy passion filling all my frame—"

To rediscover that reality can make more difference than anything to the whole of our life.

At the General Assembly of 1962, among those dedicated to special service was a Deaconess for whom this was, in a special sense, a beginning again. Some years before she had been dedicated and presented to the Moderator prior to going out to India as a Woman Missionary. After an all-too-short period of service there her health broke down completely through a form of heart trouble which meant she could never go back—indeed, she was finished, humanly speaking, for that full-time service in Christ's Church which she loved. But a famous surgeon took her in hand and performed one of those wonderful heart operations which are still so much of a marvel. After a prolonged period of recuperation she had been pronounced completely fit for anything, although it was only sensible not to go abroad. Now, with a new hope and a new life before her, she was going out afresh to Christ's Service. This is precisely the difference made when we have claimed for ourselves the birthday gift of the Church, the endowment of the Holy Spirit. We are set free from handicap, delivered from limitations, liberated into full and joyous service.

IV

THE NOTE OF URGENCY—
WE MUST LOVE HIM TOO

11

THE MASTER NEEDS OUR HELP

(A Palm Sunday Sermon)

" If anyone asks, ' Why are you doing that ? ', say, ' Our Master needs it, and will send it back here without delay '."—Mark xi. 3 (N.E.B.).

WE are looking to-day at the strange triumph of Jesus, His one and only royal procession. Suppose we try to look, just for once, not merely at the outward events themselves, but at what lay under the surface and made it all possible. In 1961 many of us must have seen, either in the cinema or on television, a film of the Royal Tour of the East. It provided a wonderful record of colourful pageantry, such as the East can provide, with cheering crowds and processions of all sorts. We saw the Queen travelling in an open car, standing up so that she could be more clearly seen. We saw her in a gorgeous horse-drawn carriage ; we even saw her perched high up on the back of an elephant as it lumbered along. Behind all the colour and the pageantry, which functioned so smoothly, lay months of painstaking planning, meticulous timing and detailed preparation so that there was the most exact dove-tailing of arrangements and precise co-operation by everyone in any way involved. It only wants someone to come too early or arrive too late ; someone fails to play his or her chosen part and everything goes wrong. The same is true of Palm Sunday, and this verse indicates clearly that the Triumphal Entry did not

simply happen, it was carefully planned by Jesus. If
He was going to die then He would die at His own
chosen time ; if Jerusalem was to cast Him out and
kill Him He would first enter the city in His own way,
giving to that entrance His own significance. There
can be no doubt that as we read between the lines of
the description in this first of the Gospels to be written
we sense the atmosphere of previous arrangement.
The disciples are given exact instructions to fit in
with a plan already fashioned in exact detail, even to
the giving of a key-password. The Authorised Version
gives this word as " the Lord hath need of him ". The
New English Bible version has a simple directness :
" Our Master needs it ". This is the justification for
the giving and the taking, this is the " key " in the
engineering sense which locks this particular cog into
its chosen place in the purpose of Jesus.

Palm Sunday sets before every one of us the
challenging and inspiring thought that Jesus Christ
needs us for the carrying out of His plan, He cannot
do without something which we can give, or do, or
be. Without that peculiar contribution that is mine
alone to make His plan miscarries ; if what He asks
and needs of me is withheld, then something is missing.
This pattern runs all through the Gospels. Constantly
we see Him needing something which men can give,
and realise that by asking for it He binds them to
Himself. He needs a place to be born when He comes
down to earth from heaven, being truly made bone of
our bone and flesh of our flesh. He finds one tiny
corner of caring and compassion and response in the
heart of a busy, bothered innkeeper who has no room
either in his " public-house " or in his own home, but
who gives a stable, a place at least of warmth, and
privacy, with a pile of straw for a birth-place and a
manger for a crib, and—Lo and behold !—what God
had planned actually works out. He is preaching to
the crowd at the side of the Sea of Galilee and they
press upon Him almost to the water's edge. He asks

Peter to pull on the mooring rope of his fishing boat, floating quietly just off shore ; He climbs on board, gets Peter to push her off again and uses the bow of the boat as a pulpit. Was that when He first began to lay hold on Peter's warm but unreliable heart ? He is sitting tired in the shade by the well of Samaria. A woman comes to draw water in the heat of the day, coming then to avoid the sly glances and gossiping tongues of her fellow-women. He asks her to draw water and give Him a drink and by asking that service makes contact with her to her eternal salvation. He needs some food to satisfy a huge crowd and a boy gives Him what was probably the remains of his own picnic lunch—could that boy ever forget the look that Jesus gave him ? He needs a young donkey to fulfil the prophecy and come as a King, yet in peace. Someone has such a beast and arranges to make it available. He needs some tiny act of love to lift His heart, to make Him feel that He can win in the end, and Mary anoints Him at Bethany. On the Via Dolorosa He stumbles under the weight of His Cross ; Simon is compelled, at first against his will, to bear the Cross, and then, surely, he lends his strong shoulder gladly. His broken body needs a tomb, and Joseph, openly loyal when it seems too late, gives it. We can see how this pattern of His needing something we can give runs through it all.

The situation is still the same. Sometimes we speak of ourselves as being mere tiny cogs in a vast impersonal machine, utterly unimportant and insignificant. Here is a heart-lifting variation on the same theme—our little lives form part of that intricate intermeshing of cogs that keep the world turning, and keep His work going, and continue to get His will done. He wants someone to teach and influence young people, realising as He does the difficulty of being young in a shaken and bewildering world. He looks to you and me to pay back something of the debt we owe for all the influences of our own youth, which have given us a compass to steer by and an anchor for the soul. Someone cries to Him in hurt or loneliness, and He looks for one of His own, living just round the corner, it may be, from that needy person, who has a little time to spare, and some caring compassion to give. We give it, and His heart lifts in joy and gratitude ; we are too busy, or we just can't be bothered, or we get out of it by saying that we are no good at that sort of thing. The need is not met and His heart is hurt and disappointed. In the changed circumstances of our modern world He calls often to us, who are His own, for some venture of faith, discipline, or obedience. " I need some of you, many of you," He says, " to give an extra of time and effort, to give at least the willingness to try. I ask you, just for once, to do something different from the ordinary run of church work and routine activity. I want your feet to walk up that path, or climb those particular stairs. I want your hands to make personal My invitation and challenge. I want your lips to pass on and share with someone else what you have been able to see in Me, in My Church, and in the life which I can offer." The basic principle underlying all the differing forms of service which He may ask of each of us is simply and gloriously that our Master needs it. He wants and needs from each of us, without exception, something that is worth giving and that from His point of view is indispensable.

The Master not only needs what we can give, He has a right to it. The N.E.B. version has an interesting footnote at the bottom of the page. For " Our Master " it gives as an alternative *or* " It's owner ". This is highly interesting and suggestive. Why should such a phrase be used in this situation ? We must try to think how it was all arranged, what may well have gone on behind the scenes. There must have been many people all over Palestine who were friendly to Jesus and we must not forget this fact when in these last days of His life His enemies prove so prominent.

He must have laid His spell upon the hearts of multitudes who had heard Him teaching and preaching and
they remained in His debt.   Then there were the very
many people whom He had healed of their various
diseases and to whom He had given a life that was
made new.   They must have been abidingly grateful,
and so would be all their friends and loved ones.   Quite
possibly, indeed very probably, the anonymous owner
of the donkey would have come among the pilgrims
from Galilee.   The road they travelled would lead right
down the valley of the Jordan to Jericho and then
back up the dangerous road to Jerusalem on its hills.
Perhaps Jesus met this man at Jericho, or elsewhere
on the way, and said to him : " I need a young donkey
like this one I see you have.   Can I have the use of it
for a little ? "   One can imagine the owner replying
immediately : " Gladly, Master.   If you can arrange
for some of the disciples to collect it, I will tell you
where it will be found, tied outside the door in the
street.   Tell them to say : ' It's owner needs it '.   You
have done so much for me and mine that all that is
mine is yours."   Here is a great abiding truth.   How
wonderfully true are the words we sing, often un-
thinkingly :

> " We give Thee but Thine own,
>   Whate'er the gift may be."

If I give a proportion of my time, some effort, a share,
however meagre, of my abilities and my material
possessions to Jesus Christ within the fellowship of
His Church it is because " It's owner needs it ".

Palm Sunday is indeed the beginning of Holy Week,
but it already calls us to look forward through the
events of each day to Good Friday.   It confronts us
with a claim upon each of us and upon all that we have
and are, a claim which we must acknowledge.   This
familiar poem is peculiarly relevant to our thought at
this point :

" They borrowed a bed to lay His head
    When Christ the Lord came down ;
They borrowed the ass in the mountain pass
    For Him to ride to town ;
But the crown that He wore and the cross that He
      bore
    Were His own—
    The cross was His own.

He borrowed the bread when the crowd He fed
    On the grassy mountain-side,
He borrowed the dish of broken fish
    With which He satisfied.
But the crown that He wore and the cross that He
      bore
    Were His own—
    The cross was His own.

He borrowed a ship in which to sit
    To teach the multitude ;
He borrowed a nest in which to rest—
    He had never a home so rude ;
But the crown that He wore and the cross that He
      bore
    Were His own—
    The cross was His own.

He borrowed a room on His way to the tomb
    The Passover Lamb to eat ;
They borrowed a cave for Him a grave,
    They borrowed a winding-sheet.
But the crown that He wore and the cross that He
      bore
    Were His own—
    The cross was His own."

Because He took on Himself the Cross that was *not* His own this fact confronts and challenges us.

What we give in response to His request and His claim we get back. The N.E.B. translates " will send it back here without delay ". There are many little points we are apt to miss, details we overlook in a story so familiar. For instance, in the *Passion Play* at Oberammergau the Palm Sunday procession is highly dramatic, with the great crowd going before and behind the figure on the donkey. When they have passed across the great stage and gone their ways, you may be quite certain that someone has been told off beforehand to take charge of the donkey, for he will be needed again at the next performance and the next. We may be sure that Jesus had not forgotten that detail, but had told off one of the disciples to take charge of the donkey and return him to his owner. From that moment, surely, that donkey was special. Just because Jesus had used him, and ridden him for a little, when he was given back he was never quite the same again. Any little child, running barefoot in the green fields of Ireland's countryside, will show you a donkey, humble beast of burden, and point out, wide-eyed, the mark of the Cross on the donkey's back. There is a great principle here which runs through the whole of life. The time we give, the abilities we use, the effort we make, the tasks to which the Master sometimes calls, sometimes compels us, pressing us into service as Simon was pressed—we get them all back. Because He needed and claimed and used this particular gift of yours and mine it becomes for ever different.

From the story of the donkey on Palm Sunday we look ahead to the morning of Good Friday, from the Triumphal Entry we look ahead to the tragic exit of Jesus from Jerusalem by the route known ever since as the Via Dolorosa. Jesus stumbles and falls under the weight of His cross. Somehow He regains His feet and staggers on. He falls again and cannot rise. Remember this is not a collapse which is purely or mainly physical. He has been under prolonged strain, nervous and emotional, such as must sap His inmost resources of strength even more than His long-drawn-out physical agony. He is bearing on His heart the sin of the world, for He cannot take away that sin unless He takes it into His own heart. He most desperately needs a strong shoulder, needs this more than He has needed, all His life, any service which can humanly be given. The centurion in charge of the execution squad looks round quickly and from the crowd singles out Simon of Cyrene. He just happened to be there, at that exact spot, at that precise moment. He was there for his own reasons, bent on his own personal purposes, and he cannot have enjoyed being thus singled out. It would be surprising if his first reaction were not to feel bitter, rebellious, and resentful, asking angrily : " Why did this have to happen to me ? " But surely this first feeling changed as he went on, settling the weight of the ugly cross on his own strong shoulder. Did Jesus, even in this most unlikely moment, still exert His strange grip on the soul of man, and claim Simon, contrary to all expectations ? When they came to Calvary itself and Simon's resentful task was completed, did he just drop the cross and hurry away back to his own business, whatever it was, or did he stay to the end, gripped and held by the strange Figure on the Cross ? Both Mark and Paul hint that the sons and wife of this Simon became well known in the Church. It would be strange if he, too, did not come to be numbered among the followers of this haunting Jesus. Perhaps years after the Crucifixion and the Resurrection Simon would rub his shoulder reflectively, hardly conscious that he was doing it, remembering how on the morning of that dark day the Master needed Simon's strength, and claimed it and used it, and then gave it back, for ever enriched. Truly the man who gave the gift which the Master, its Owner, so badly needed had his own reward.

12

THE MASTER TRUSTS US GREATLY

" To every man according to his several ability."—Matt. xxv. 15.

THIS very familiar story provides an interesting instance of the kind of difference made by the New English Bible translation. Set it alongside the Authorised Version in the case of this particular story, and the very first point which strikes you is the loss in the N.E.B. of a word which has found a very prominent place in the English language and in our thinking, for the word " talent " is dropped altogether. We have come to use the idea of talents in the sense of special gifts in the realm of the arts, where we can talk of a young pianist of special talent ; in the world of sport, where we speak of the " talent-spotters " being out in force at a game ; and in the entertainment world where we can describe a particular actress as showing unexpected talent in a " straight part ". The N.E.B. version uses " bags of gold ", which is what the " talents " really were, but the result is to give a rather over-specialised meaning and an application to the story which is very limited. Bags of gold were indeed the actual entrustment in the original story, but we cannot help applying the message of the story much more widely to refer to natural gifts, endowments and abilities, all special in kind or degree and given to certain individuals in differing measure. Even here we are tempted to become over-specialised and to limit dangerously the application of a great message. The vast majority of us who make up the bulk of the membership of the Holy Catholic Church would never claim to be particularly " talented " and this both lets us out and leaves us out of a great idea

with a peculiar inspiration for every one of us without
exception. If the word " talents " called for re-
translation, the story calls even more urgently for
re-examination.

This story sets before us the principle of trust, a
wonderfully challenging and inspiring idea. This is
made quite clear by the story itself, but it is insuffi-
ciently realised. The N.E.B. version makes this clear
by saying that the owner puts his " capital ", all of it,
in the hands of his servants. He puts his whole estate
in their care. Then he leaves them to it, he goes
away, not just a few miles, where he will know obviously what is happening, and where they can call on
him in an emergency, but to a far country. Not only
so, he stays away a long time, until they must have
been tempted to think he was never coming back.
He does not lay down strict regulations as to how his
capital is to be used, with every detail carefully covered.
He trusts them completely and leaves the use of his
money to their own judgment. This is a picture of
life as we know it to be. This is exactly the way God
runs His world. In theory, at least, it could have
been different. One of the Psalms takes up and
develops this possibility and pictures God as saying :
" If I were hungry, I would not tell thee ", reminding
us that the whole creation is God's to do with exactly
as He may choose. Presumably God could have
created a world which was one vast machine, completely and mechanically perfect, each part smoothly
interlocking, with nothing to go wrong, and no part
dangerously possessed of any will of its own. He
could have made life like a vast chess-board, with
men as His pawns, moved from place to place or discarded in some fantastic game of His right hand
against His left. He could have made us like puppets,
to dance always and only as He pulled the strings.
But no ! God be praised ! He leaves us on our own.
He sets us free to run or ruin His world ; to shatter or
to strengthen and support His plan. It is not that

He does not care, that it is not important enough to Him what we may do with His world. The whole story of Jesus Christ can be summed up in the one great phrase : " God so loved the world ". On the Cross Christ has taken this world of ours for better, for worse. In a great phrase of the late Dr. John White : " God has put too much of Himself into the world to desert it now ".

None the less He has chosen to hold His hand and leave us to it. What this must cost God we may not know but we can at least try to understand. A mother has a young daughter who is anxious, sometimes over-anxious, to help, it may be with washing or with sewing. It would be easier, far easier for the mother to do it herself rather than let her daughter learn, by making mistakes, often costly mistakes, so that she must stand by and see some valued fabric spoiled by wrong washing or some piece of delicate embroidery done so badly that it has to be taken out and done again. If the mother can be great enough in patience and in trust then, then only the daughter can really learn. There can be little doubt that this is how Jesus was treated in the carpenter's shop at Nazareth. Although even He must on occasion have cut Himself and spoiled some piece of wood, yet Joseph helped Him by letting Him do things on His own so that He was learning by being trusted, and seeing, in the process, how our Heavenly Father trusts us. Or, to take a perhaps painful illustration, how difficult it is to teach someone of your own to drive, especially on your own new car ! It is said that a man can teach his fiancée to drive but not his wife ! The temptation to take over and end your own agony is almost irre-sistible. What must God feel as He watches us spoiling His plans and ruining His world. Yet He insists on going on trusting us. There is a famous legend which describes a meeting between the Archangel Gabriel and the Risen Lord after the Ascension. Gabriel looking at the marks of the thorns on the Master's brow exclaims : " Master, you have suffered ". " Yes, Gabriel, I have suffered." Then Gabriel, looking at the wounds in the hands of Jesus, goes on : " And, Master, you have died ". " Yes, Gabriel, I have died." " Master, what have you done to make sure that the cause for which you suffered and died will go on ? " " Well, Gabriel, I have told Peter and Andrew and James and John and the rest and told them to go and tell others." Gabriel, not sharing the Lord's faith in our fallible human nature, carries his questioning a stage further. " But, Master, what if they do not do it ? What if Peter denies you again and the others desert as they did before ? What then, Master ? " To which the Lord replies quite simply : " Nothing, then, Gabriel. I am trusting them." None of us are left out, all of us are in this wonderful, challenging relationship of trust.

The story leads on to the second principle, that of variations of entrustment. In the parallel story of the Pounds, each servant is given exactly the same ; here all are different. This is life as we know it to be, for there are undoubtedly wide differences of native endowment. How unequal men are in their equipment for life ; in the way of health, brains, or special genius or capacity ! One boy is born a Yehudi Menuhin with music in his very soul and a wonderful capacity to give joy to others ; another is tone deaf and music means nothing to him. How very much in life is pretty well decided by the accident of birth and environment. One girl is born with the gifts and opportunities which send her to boarding school and then to finishing school in Switzerland ; another ends her limited education in a restless, resentful final year at a Junior Secondary School. Such accidents of birth and surroundings have far more to do than we normally realise with the possession of a real religion or the utter lack of it ; they can decide whether I am a Roman Catholic or a Presbyterian or nothing at all. We are coming to realise more and more how much they have to do with basic realities, such as plain goodness or badness. Listening to evidence from Probation Officers, Chief Constables, Chaplains, Prison and Borstal Governors in connection with the Scottish Advisory Council on the Treatment of Offenders I become more and more impressed with the fact that there are types of area which produce more than the normal quota of crime and delinquency, and that there is an undoubted connection between both of these evils and a low intellectual capacity. There are, indeed, obvious and dramatic contrasts in the gifts and endowments, the opportunities and chances given to each of us. This is the situation frankly faced in our story where the " talents " are given in the proportion of five, two and one.

At the same time it is well to remember that there is a wider interpretation of the situation that is also true. There are gifts which are given to all of us. There is life itself, that precious gift without which all others have no meaning. There is time, however limited, and are there not twenty-four hours in the day for us all, be we wise or simple, rich or poor ? There is some ability, however meagre, given to each and all of us. In the so-called " affluent society " it is becoming more and more true that ordinary people have some share of material possessions. We may not have, in terms of the N.E.B. translation, " bags " of money but most of us have some ! Money is important not for itself but for what it can do, a fact which is increasingly obscured by our mixed-up scales of values. In a large house in a lovely suburban district of one of our cities there lived for several years a lonely, frustrated and rather embittered woman. She had inherited considerable wealth from her dead husband, to whom she was deeply attached. From the time of his death to her own she lived by herself, afraid to spend the money even on herself, completely self-centred in a world filled with self-pity. What a waste it all seemed, for there was so much good she might have done, so much joy she might have given, and so much deep happiness she might have found in the giving. Hers was the waste of a trust betrayed and an opportunity neglected. In her case this was dramatically obvious, but it is true of every one of us. We are all in this, for in the story there was no one to whom nothing was given.

This truth is very hard to accept. We have, every one of us, some part, however humble, in this venture of trust. It is most significant that the one-talent man is subject to the gravest temptation. Those of us who have only one talent, if that, are so much aware of our limitations. What matters is what we do about these limitations. We may resent them, and nurse a grudge against life because we were given only one talent. We may be jealous of those who were given five and two and shrug off all responsibility, saying : " Let them get on with it ". We may take refuge behind our limitations, and this attitude is by far the most common. There is no single influence that cripples any effort of a special kind and leaves the normal work of the Church so pathetically short of its potential as this widespread reaction which insists : " There is nothing I can do, there will be plenty without me ". In the average congregation perhaps one-eighth consists of people with five talents or two and they are frequently left with most of the responsibility. In a sense this is right and proper, for it is true particularly of them that " to whom much is given, of him much will be required ". If there are five- and two-talent people doing nothing in their church then a grave responsibility for the ineffectiveness of the Church lies at their door. But there are the other seven-eighths who are one-talent men and women and the great continuing task, in every congregation without exception, is to mobilise and harness their possibilities. The same is true of the whole Church and it is true also of the world. God must believe most passionately in one-talent people for He has

made so many of them.   If God made us as we are
then none of us can ever be " a nobody " for God has
no time to make nobodies.

It is very revealing that the excuse given by the one-
talent man for his failure to trade with the talent
entrusted to him was quite simply : " I was afraid ".
One of the most encouraging aspects of the Christian
Stewardship movement is that it has come to so many
ordinary, average men and women in the Church and
enabled them to get over their fears and set aside their
excuses.   It has reminded them that, however poorly
we may be endowed, and however limited the opportunities given to us, we are all immeasurably in God's
debt for life itself and for all His gifts to us in Christ.
Each of us must make some response.   By widening
the scope of opportunities for Christian service and
using imaginatively the possibilities which ordinary
people actually possess, this movement has said,
pointedly and personally, and in a new way to very
many : " There is something you can do, and there is
something you should be doing ".   By making us face
this challenge of opportunity, and by encouraging us
even to try doing something difficult, this new approach
to Christian service has given a new thrill to ordinary
people of all sorts, the thrill of discovering that I can
do more than I dared to think, and given to us the joy
of knowing that we were being used, that Christ has
not trusted us in vain.

So we pass to the wonderful principle of equal
reward for equal trustworthiness.   This is the final
heart-lifting feature of this old and familiar story, the
two faithful servants are addressed in precisely the
same way, and are called in exactly similar terms to
share in the greater trust for which they have proved
themselves to be so well fitted.   This is surely a
splendid incentive, that equal faithfulness wins an
exactly equal reward.   The abiding impression left
by the story of these men who are trusted in differing
degrees, " every man according to his several ability ",

is that to whom much is given, of him much will be required. There is therefore no need to be jealous, no occasion for the two-talent man to be envious of his neighbour gifted with five talents, or to excuse inactivity on his own part by dreaming of what he might have done if their positions had been reversed. It seems that the degree of our entrustment is exactly matched to our capabilities ; we are not asked to do any more or less than realise our own personal potential. But who judges and determines beforehand what is the capacity, who estimates with clear understanding and sure vision the personal potential of each of us ? Surely the message of the story is that the Master does this. When we apply the message of the story to ourselves this fact takes on new meaning, for the Master and Owner with whom we have to deal and to whom we are responsible is also our Maker and Preserver. Here is a further application of the familiar lines of Robert Burns :

> " Who made the heart, 'tis He alone
>   Decidedly can try us."

Can we doubt the wisdom of His judgment, or suggest that He ever trusts us unfairly ? The only one of the three men in the story who is condemned is the one who failed to come up to the Master's estimate of his capabilities.

This is the sin of sins, not just to be positively wicked, but to fail to realise our God-given possibilities, to " let God down " by neglecting to be and do what, by His endowment and on His estimate of us we have it in us to be and do. What a stark and inescapable challenge this is for every Christian. It is easy to realise the cogency of this truth in the case of some outstanding examples. The story of Sir Alexander Fleming, the discoverer of penicillin, is a case in point. All through his story, his going to London, his turning to medicine as a career, his specialising in chemistry, at every turn one is left with the feeling of a chance which was really choice and of the guiding hand of an over-ruling providence. The " discovery " itself, the growth of that particular culture out of all the possibilities that were open, his noticing what had happened and recognising instinctively the meaning which it carried, all these are signs of the ways in which God can use His exceptionally talented servants for the lasting benefit of mankind. Thinking over that story I could not help recalling a visit paid many years ago to a lace works in the village of Darvel within a mile or two of the farm where Fleming was born and brought up. Lace curtains were being made on a loom which could work with two different kinds of thread and several colours. The manager explained to me that the different shuttles came into operation according to a pattern carefully worked out on a perforated card. High up above the machine was fixed what is called " the harness ", and from it cords lead down through the perforations to the various shuttles. As the machine works each cord in turn, pulling from above, releases the proper shuttle that it may play its part in working out the pattern, both of differing threads and various colours. One can clearly see in the life of a Fleming the purposes from above being worked out stage by stage. It is not so easy to see it in our own lives, yet of each of us, too, it is gloriously true I can put in my one thread in the pattern, and in so doing live up to God's estimate of my potential and justify the great trust of God.

13

THE MASTER LOOKS ON YOUTH

" Jesus looked straight at him ; his heart warmed to him, and he said, ' One thing you lack '."—Mark x. 21 (N.E.B.).

THE Authorised Version of this text states simply that Jesus " loved him " and that is surely great enough. Of course, we know that Jesus loves everyone, for He died in love for all men, yet there are some who are specially mentioned in relation to His love. It is striking that on only three occasions is it stated of an individual in the Gospels that Jesus loved this person. We read, for example, " Now Jesus loved Martha ", which is not surprising. She and her family had been drawn very close to Jesus by what He did for them, and what their love did in return for Him. It would have been strange had He not grown to love them in a special degree. John is described as " the disciple whom Jesus loved ", and, of course, John had a long association with Jesus, in a special way he had proved himself a kindred spirit, he and the Master must have been very close in mind and heart. But it also stands written that Jesus loved this man, this stranger, who is and remains anonymous. This is surprising and striking, and the New English Bible translation brings it out when it says that " his heart warmed to him ". The man came running up, and bursting in on Jesus in his eagerness; he asked his anxious question about eternal life and was given his answer in Jesus' own inimitable fashion. But he was obviously not satisfied ; his question might be answered but *he* was not ; he wanted more. That is when we read that " Jesus looked straight at him " ; He looked at him right between the eyes with this astonishing and often uncomfortable knack He possessed of seeing right to the heart of another human being. Seeing there what He alone could see, His heart warmed to His questioner. One gets the impression of a spark leaping the gap between these two persons, of a fire kindled between them, and it is wonderful that this should happen. It still can and does happen, even now when we meet in the name and in the living presence of Jesus Christ, for He is still the same ; He still sees to the heart of each of us, His heart still warms in glad response to what He finds.

His heart goes out in joyful recognition of possibilities. The whole idea of the warm-hearted response of Jesus to what He insists on seeing in our much-maligned human personality is of the widest possible application. At the same time the story itself gives a particular direction to our thinking. The other Gospel accounts tell us that the anonymous questioner was young. Jesus, looking on him, saw him clean and fine and eager and full of promise ; saw someone not asking any idle, theoretical question but genuinely wanting, deeply longing to make the most of life. How often Jesus must see youth like that, though we too often forget it. It is high time we listened to this same Jesus speaking up in defence of youth. Amid all our rightful concern for the youth of to-day, it is dangerously easy to speak as if young people were all juvenile delinquents, actual or potential. We become so obsessed with the misdemeanours of some of our youth that we talk as if to be a " teenager " is a crime or a disease or both ! While we may honestly lament the undoubted increase in laxity of sexual behaviour, we must not presume to conclude that the morals of all or most of our young people are those of the barn-yard. It is dangerously easy, in the heat of our concern, to tie on large masses of our youth labels like " teddy-boy ", " beatnik type " and so on, and to ascribe to all those thus labelled all the worst characteristics we associate with that title.

It is more than time we set about deliberately

trying to rediscover what Jesus sees when the Master looks on youth to-day. Does He see their honesty, their frankness, their determination to face the facts of life, whether we give to that phrase its usual very limited meaning (as if there were no other " facts " in life than those connected with sex) or a wider connotation ? And does He find this honesty, which so embarrasses us, far better and healthier than the humbug and hypocrisy which were so much part of the " Victorian " attitude ? Does His heart warm when He senses their capacity for enthusiasm even when they would fall over backwards to protest their lack of enthusiasm for anything ? Does He rejoice to sense their hot anger at evils we, who are older, have far too long accepted as inevitable ; their deep-seated concern about such evils, and their insistent demand that something should be done ? Does it gladden His heart to see them trying to do something, however extreme the methods they use, about War on Want or Nuclear Disarmament ? Surely the hymn-writer is on sound lines when he speaks of Jesus and describes

" Kind eyes that marked the lilies in their beauty,
    And heart that kindled at the zeal of youth."

It is high time we stopped saying to our young people, simply : " You mustn't, you shouldn't . . .", when the only reason we can give to justify this attitude is : " We didn't " ! It is time we set about, seriously and sympathetically, not only giving to them but setting them clear standards of right and wrong. It is most important that we should do this without any suggestion of merely " laying down the law " to them ; rather should we make it plain that this is the way to make life work, just as, in another setting, we might say : " If you want to bake a birthday cake that is a success, or to sew a party dress that will not look home-made, or to drive a car really well, or to sail a small boat in a choppy sea, then this is the way to do it ". We must learn again to look on youth in terms of possibilities, for this is the way Jesus sees them. In spite of all our failures with youth, and the large numbers whom the Church misses completely, there must still be many occasions when the heart of Jesus warms to what He sees. Here is a group of young people who do everything together ; they have gone to the same school together, grown up in uniformed organisations together ; played games together ; and here they gather in the hall of their church on a Sunday evening to think out seriously and reverently what it means for them to follow Christ together, and to discover what they may do for His sake together. Surely the heart of Christ must warm. Here is a great church filled with Boy Scouts for their Annual Parade ; their ages eleven to eighteen, all alike having made originally and that day solemnly renewing a promise which accepts duty to be done, service to be rendered, and laws to be kept. Is not this an encouragement to the heart of Him who died upon a Cross as the young Prince of Glory ? At the Candlelight Service at 11.30 on Christmas Eve in St. Cuthbert's Church, Edinburgh, the church is usually crowded to overflowing with a congregation of between fifteen hundred and two thousand, and at least seventy-five per cent are young people. They come from the cinema, the dance hall, from the skating rink with their skates still over their shoulders ; they come, some of them, in their teddy-boy suits, the girls in their slacks and head-squares ; they come, others of them, in evening dress from a dinner-dance. In spite of all these many variations I feel sure that the heart of Jesus warms to them, seeing them, all, without exception, in terms of their possibilities.

The heart of the Master warms to youth in searching understanding. If we underline the phrase in the text which tells that Jesus " looked straight at him " that can remind us how Jesus sees right home to the heart of the situation confronting youth to-day. No psychiatrist with all his accumulated knowledge and specialised techniques could have gone deeper or read the situation more truly. Jesus saw all that His questioner possessed—wealth, health, his clean youth, his correct behaviour. He saw also that, with all these, the young man was not satisfied, he was looking for something more, even if he did not himself realise what he was seeking. Jesus knew He must be honest with him ; he truly wanted an answer and would not be put off. Indeed, the worst injustice that could be done to him would be to attempt to put him off. This is precisely the real situation confronting youth to-day ; they are looking, most of them, for something they have not found ; and we older people, especially in the Church, must try to see that with real understanding. Vast numbers of our young people are looking, perhaps without realising that they are doing so, for a life that has worth, meaning, importance, and purpose. They are not finding it, but they keep on looking, sometimes with a wistful sort of eagerness and persistence.

Sometimes this failure to find a worthwhile and satisfying way of life is occasioned for our young people by handicapping circumstances. If a lad has left school at fifteen, been in half-a-dozen dead-end jobs before he is eighteen, become unemployed then and been in danger of becoming unemployable by the time he is twenty-one, what chance is there of him seeing life as a worthwhile and meaningful business, to which he can make an important personal contribution ? This restless searching for something never found, hankering after a purpose never realised, really explains many of the " odd " things some of our young people do ; their striving after self-expression in dress and hair-style (which is equally true of both sexes !). It also explains some of their silly extravagances of conduct which shock and mystify an older generation. When teenage girls scream and shriek over some " pop " singer or film star, this is only a misguided expression of the longing to have

someone to admire, someone to whom they can give
their total loyalty, an expression which is pathetic
because of its lack of a truly worthy object of such
devotion. This, too, explains something of the tremendous cult of sport in all its forms, whether for the
participant or the spectator—here is one answer to
the longing for a thrill, a purpose, a cause in which
you can lose yourself. When the fervent Supporters'
Clubs of Glasgow Rangers F.C., so many of them
young men and women, sing their theme song " Follow,
follow, we will follow Rangers ", they never realise
that the words are a parody of one of the old Revivalist
hymns, and that their very enthusiasm is perhaps a
parody of zeal for a cause far greater. When young
girls indulge in promiscuous sexual adventure, does
this spring, perhaps, from a longing to be wanted by
someone, even if it means being " wanted " only on
this level, and leads to a vicious circle of ever deeper
frustration ? In dealing with youth, especially in the
Church of this warm-hearted Master, there is con-
tinual need for understanding all through and at every
stage. No one can really meet the needs of youth
to-day who does not reckon adequately with their
sense, however vague and incoherent, of having
missed the meaning of life, been denied something,
possessing an empty, aching place that is never quite
filled. Amid all the lavish entertainment, and the
many things which higher wages make available to
youth to-day, it is as true as ever that

> " From the best bliss that earth imparts
>   We turn unfilled to Thee again."

When the Master looks on youth His heart warms in
caring compassion. That day long ago Jesus presented
an inescapable challenge, He put His finger unerringly
on the weak spot, the sensitive spot, and that fine
young man winced. His face fell, and he went away
with a heavy heart. He could not face it ; he was not
prepared to pay the price of accepting the answer for

which he had asked so eagerly. As he turned away, his steps dragging reluctantly, the heart of Jesus warmed to him in a compassion which sprang from His deep understanding of the young man's true situation. He is still the same ; His heart still goes out to young people. We read in the Gospels that He looked with compassion on the crowd because they were " as sheep not having a shepherd ". Surely He must look with equal compassion upon the great masses of our young people of whose real condition it would be an under-statement to say that they are " as sheep not having a shepherd ". How many among them—the vast majority, indeed—left school at fifteen, probably gladly and eagerly, going out into the real world, to earn real money, and really to begin living. Now they are only in their late teens and already at a loose end, even if some of them are married and with a family before they are twenty. How many of the young men are destined or doomed already, partly by the economic circumstances of their upbringing, partly by their own failure to have made the best of their opportunities and possibilities, to be nothing more or less than a general labourer all their working days. Even if a general labourer is now paid much more highly than a tradesman and craftsman used to be, this cannot make for a really inspiring " daily round and common task ".

Or what, less obviously perhaps, of the luckier ones, those who were given the benefit of a higher education, the people who are " salaried " rather than " wage-earning ", who have suffered, within their own setting, from the general lowering of standards and loss of clear conviction ? What of the young people, and not least the young couples, settling down in their own homes, paying off the bond on the house, busy " keeping up with the Jones's ", knowing only what they do not believe, with no vital faith to give meaning and purpose to their many activities and to set great horizons about what is, for all its comfort and its equipment of gadgets,

a very little life ? Many of them, indeed most, have
had at least a nominal, if largely superstitious connection with the Church, through their own baptism, their
marriage in a church building, probably even the
baptism of their own children. On all of these occasions,
though they may not have realised it, their lives for a
little were focused on Jesus Christ, for a fleeting
moment He had just the glimmering of a chance to
break through to them. How His heart must warm
in compassion and caring, knowing as He does how
much they are missing.

Nor must we confine this thought of the compassion
of Christ merely, if mainly, to the young. There is
just as real a problem with people in middle age, with
the first glad strength of youth gone, just when the
burdens of responsibility are getting heavier ; many
of them, no doubt, reasonably comfortable and leading
apparently successful lives, as the world counts success,
yet these lives are not linked to anything truly worth
while. So very many of them fully merit, although
they might protest that it is not so, the description in
Myers' *St. Paul*.

" Bound who should conquer, slaves who should be
      kings."

Or what of the " forgotten generation ", the old
people who may well feel utterly lost and bewildered
in such a world as this, and are sometimes given excuse
for imagining that they are not wanted ? To all of us
alike, in every generation, Jesus Christ keeps coming
again, setting before us the answer to our questions,
pointing us to the only true end of man's age-long
search. Still the story of this young man is rewritten ;
we ask, and are given our answer, but we refuse to
accept it, or we cannot pay the price. We may be
young and are looking for life that will be life indeed.
Christ tells us how we can have it now and keep it
always, on His conditions. But we will not accept His
discipline, we want a good time first. Or we are in the

middle years, troubled by vague discontent, conscious that we may not have a great deal of time left to go on searching. He brings us to the end of our quest but insists that we give up something and we cannot do it. Or, perhaps, we are old ; we have seen everything there is in life ; we keep hankering after the return of old dead days beyond recall. He leads us, even us, to the verge of new discoveries in the business of living, but we will not have it. Yet, amid it all, His heart still warms to us, insisting on seeing us, even yet, in terms of possibilities ; His heart warms to us every one, both in searching understanding and caring compassion.

14

THE FINAL TEST OF REALITY IN
RELIGION

" Inasmuch as ye have done it unto one of the least of these
my brethren, ye have done it unto me."—Matt. xxv. 40.

ON the end wall of the Sistine Chapel in the Vatican
at Rome there is one of the world's great mural
paintings. The whole roof is covered in marvellous
detail with other paintings by Michelangelo and one
wonders why, with all this beauty leading the eye
upwards, the artist should have chosen to add this
vast painting on the end wall. Most probably it was
because towards that wall everyone looked inevitably.
This was the focal point of all the worship offered in
the Chapel ; the eye, the heart, and the soul were led
to the altar, and the Cross and then to this picture
rising and soaring above and beyond. It seems that
the artist deliberately took the story of the Last
Judgment which comes at the very end of all the
teaching of Jesus and painted it in this position so
that it would always be there, at least in the background of all the thinking and the worshipping of
those who came to the Sistine Chapel. Nothing could
be more challenging and salutary for the widely varied
work of any modern congregation than to take this
same story and make it the back-cloth of our every
action and of every aspect of our church's life. As
we think of the response to which we are continually
called, as we listen to the message of the gospel, and
look reverently towards the Cross, let us take this
familiar story, the words of which we know off by
heart, and put it back in its place that we may look at
all we do as Christians in the setting of this picture.
To do this effectively let us do in imagination what

can be done so helpfully with a television camera, first taking " a wide shot " to see the sweep and meaning of the whole picture, and then " swinging " to a telescopic lens and bringing near particular details.

Here is Jesus' own test of the reality and validity of the worship, work, and witness of every congregation and of the individuals who compose it. This constitutes an all-in judgment from which no one can ever be exempt. Before the King are gathered all nations, all sorts and conditions of men. They are divided into the sheep and goats and there is only one distinction which is recognised. It is staggeringly different from all our accepted and expected criteria. Jesus was telling this story in the courts of the Temple, and the very physical arrangement of the various courts divided men into Jews and Gentiles, devout or careless, sacred or secular. What mattered more than anything at that moment to His hearers was to offer the correct sacrifices and to bring the prescribed offerings which made a man right with God and assured his eternal welfare. The crowds gathered for the Passover in Jerusalem must have been utterly startled at this picture which Jesus drew. How can we ever translate that sense of shocked surprise ? When you and I go to our accounting, when the books are opened and the record of each of us is checked, what is the Judge going to ask and what am I going to answer ? He is going to ask quite simply what I did with the life He entrusted to me. What answer do I feel I would be prepared to give ? " I was brought up in a Christian home, I was given a wide variety of Christian training, I played my part, admittedly not as well as I might, in all the life and activity of the church. In my own church, which was very dear to me, I sat in the same seat for fifty years (and woe betide any misguided visitor who tried to usurp it !). I gave as I thought I was able for many good causes." Then the King will take me up on what I am saying : " But all these that you are quoting are privileges you enjoyed. What did you do with them, what kind of person did you become because of them, what spirit of practical caring and concern did you show for the least of these, my brethren ? " This according to Jesus is the only distinction that will matter, this alone will be recognised at the final accounting.

Here and now we are, beyond all question, deeply and widely divided. We are divided by the amount of money we earn or inherit, by the type of house we live in, by the work through which we earn our daily bread, by our " status " in society, by the degree and kind of education we have been given, by our differing abilities, by the fact of being good, bad or indifferent, by our success or failure in conforming to the standards of behaviour set by and accepted in the community within which our lot is set. In the last resort, Jesus insists, only this one division will count, and it will completely cancel out all the other differences. The dividing line will be simply this " inasmuch as ye did it, inasmuch as ye did it not unto one of the least of these my brethren ". Part of the fascination of the popular TV programme *What's my Line?* lies in the way it helps us to realise the very wide variation of work which ordinary people may be doing from day to day. There are two questions which the panel hardly ever fail to ask. " Is there an end product ? Is this a service ? " These are precisely the searching questions which Jesus, through this picture of the Last Judgment, keeps posing for all our church life. Our finances may be " on the up-and-up ", the attendances at church may be on the increase, the halls may be a a hive of activity all the week, but He will persistently refuse to be impressed, unless and until we have faced the question : " Is there an end-product of all this ? ", and the further question which indicates the kind of end-product for which He will always look : " Is this a service ? "

On a visit to Newcastle a year or two ago I was told

of a man, a keen church member, who had died with tragic suddenness. Men were still, in their own way, " writing his obituary ", in other words, remarking upon what they remembered of him with affection and esteem. They remembered that for fifty years he had been a business man of utter integrity, exercising an ever-increasing influence in his chosen profession. They remembered that for forty of these years he had been an Elder and for most of them Session Clerk in the church that he loved. But what they remembered most was that for the last year of his life he had got up half an hour earlier than he need do and gone round by the home of an old couple with no help, cleaned out the fireplace, lit the fire, and made their breakfast ready, before he went to his office. No one will question that it will be important when the books of his life are made up that he exercised that influence in the community and served thus lovingly and faithfully in the Church of His Lord. But, if Jesus' teaching is to be taken seriously, the most important part of his record will be : " Inasmuch as ye have done it unto these two of the least of my brethren, ye have done it unto me ".

Here is a challenge to the stewardship of our opportunities. This point is not specifically mentioned in any of the generally accepted definitions of Christian Stewardship but in a sense it is the common denominator of them all. " Opportunity ", by its derivation, means literally " that which lies at our door ". Both the types of people described in the picture of the Last Judgment had lived in the actual setting of those who are hungry, thirsty, sick, and in prison. Neither of them attempted to deny or protest that around them had been some or all of the types mentioned in the list. All alike had been called to live their lives in a setting of real need. Some had noticed that need, at one point or another ; they had taken it to their own hearts, in some degree ; they had done something in terms of caring. The others had not noticed,

or not cared, or at least not cared enough to do anything about it.

The actual mural painting in the Sistine Chapel is
in a sense up in the air, and this message of the story
of the Last Judgment may well suffer from being left
there, up in the air. We badly need to bring its
teaching down to earth in terms of practical situations.
If we take " opportunity " in its literal sense, what
need lies at your door and mine ? It will not do to
take this too literally for opportunity can occur in
subtle ways. There may be opportunities presented
to us in the neighbourhood in which we live, on the
road to or from our daily work, at that work itself,
even in a wider sense within the church to which we
belong, or the kind of community which is ours. Take
the detailed list given by Jesus and go down it with
some imagination. Think, for example, how many
lonely people there are, with the increasing urbanisa-
tion of society. How acutely lonely one can be in a
crowd. How easy it is to feel " the odd one out ",
not least in a crowd of gay young people. Is there any
form of being " sick " which can bring as much heartbreak as being acutely homesick ? In a city like
Edinburgh what about the many " strangers " who
come from lands afar to study or to work in our
midst ? While we would strenuously deny any suggestion of colour bar, what an opportunity is missed
of taking in such visitors, who are sensitive and forming
lasting impressions, right or wrong. Under the pressures of modern living nearly all of us rub shoulders,
day and daily, with someone who is frustrated, actually
hurt or pathetically " bruisable ", or who is shut in a
prison-house of self, of fear, or of bitterness.

It is surprising and encouraging what can be done
in the way of caring, practical service, given a little
imagination and the willingness to use the opportunities which are actually presented. A little American
magazine called *Guideposts* carries a regular feature
entitled " The Quiet People ", which tells the real-life

stories of simple folk who do inestimable good in quiet ways. One example will suffice. It is the story of a woman who exercises a healing ministry by simply writing letters. She has built up a list of people who might not have anyone to write to them, children in orphan homes, patients in hospital far away from home, certain prisoners serving their sentences and utterly discarded by their " ain folk ". By writing to them regularly she maintains contact and makes them feel that someone is interested enough to care. The Commitment Card issued in most Christian Stewardship Campaigns contains a list of forms of service which may be rendered, directly in the church, or outside it in the community. If one could make up a composite list from all such cards issued in the wide variety of congregations it would be seen clearly that there are all sorts of jobs to be done. I am sure that in the Church as a whole, and in every individual congregation, whatever its nature and situation, there is a tremendous potential of practical, caring, compassionate service which has never been anything like realised. We fall far short of that potential for two main reasons ; first, because we do not notice the need, and, second, because we lack the imagination to realise the importance and value of what each of us might do in direct and simple ways. None of us are left out of this, there is something everyone of us can do. Suppose we start looking now, just noticing some need that is there already, at my door, and that constitutes my personal and peculiar opportunity.

Here is, above all, a glorious suggestion of a way in which we can show our love and gratitude to Christ. There is a lovely, heart-warming detail in this great picture of the Last Judgment, which may easily go unnoticed. It is the description of the way in which the righteous react to being thus highly honoured by the King. They do not at all take it for granted. They do not, in effect, declare by their attitude : " This is just what we expected. This is what we did it for. Any service we rendered was to acquire merit. Anything less than such a reward would have been most unjust." On the contrary, they all protest that this honour is being done to them on false pretences ; this must be a case of mistaken identity. There can be no denying the air of complete mystification, and almost violent protest with which they exclaim : " Lord, when saw we Thee sick . . . and came unto Thee ? " It is only against the background of this, their very real feeling of surprise and protest, that we can even begin to appreciate their wonder and joy when the King replies : " Inasmuch as ye have done it unto one of the least of these my brethren, ye have done it unto me ".

What a wonderful idea, and what an entirely lovely suggestion. We all know people with whom you can never get even ; they will never let you give them anything, although you are often and deeply in their debt. How does one ever get through to express love and gratitude to someone who has everything already, and who will not give you the slightest chance to " get even " ? This can involve very real frustration, and deny us one of the great joys of living. In that delightful novel *The Dean's Watch*, by Elizabeth Goudge, one of the loveliest passages describes the developing friendship between the Dean, public figure and great dignitary of the Church, and Bella, the little girl who takes such firm hold of his heart with her small but very determined fingers. The Dean wants to give Bella something, but he has no idea of the real desires of little girls like Bella. He consults the lady in a likely shop, putting his problem and gaining her sympathy. She makes various suggestions but none seem to him to be entirely suitable. Then the suggestion is made of a child's umbrella, little more than a toy yet real and made to scale. The Dean is delighted, chooses his colour carefully, and sets off clutching his precious parcel, finding the rare joy of giving to someone he loves a gift which will be the very thing she wanted. This is precisely the quality of joy, and the depth of satisfaction which this story holds out before us all. Any effort of Christian service in any of the varied fields suggested by the details of this picture of the Last Judgment, according to the words of Jesus Himself, is " the very thing He wants ". By rendering this kind of simple, direct, practical service we are getting done what Christ wants done, and to know that this is true is to find, in a rare degree, the joy of being used in the way of His purpose, and bringing the light of gladness to His eyes.

There is one further by-product of this opportunity to show our love and gratitude to Christ. It saves us from the frustrating and debilitating sense of helplessness which is so trying a feature of modern life, and, not least, of Christian living in such a world as this. The trouble and tragedy of life to-day is that there are so many situations of hurt or wrong about which we can do little or nothing. We are made aware, through films and television, as we sit in our own homes, enjoying such comfort and security as may be ours, of the extent to which hunger, homelessness, despair, disease, wars and rumours of war are the inescapable realities for multitudes of our fellow-human beings. We do not have the chance any longer simply to put these things out of our minds. The place-names, the geographical locations may change, but the essential tragedies remain the same—Cuba, Laos, the Congo, the Gaza Strip, Algeria—the list goes on and there is really nothing we ordinary people can do about it. Oh yes, we can give our money, but we feel it is not enough ; this may mean no more than " aspirin " to deaden the pain of being a Christian man or woman living in the same world with such desperate human need. All this is very bad for us. That is why I, personally, like many another minister, am thankful for the week's round of hospital visits, for it brings one face to face with the problem of human suffering at the personal level ; it challenges me with the courage, the patience, and the faith of real people, as they deal with their share of this vast problem. It takes a little of the problem from me if I am allowed to share in any degree in bearing their burden with them. This is only one instance of a need which can and should be met much more widely, the need to do something, something positive and something that will make a difference, however small, to the burden of the world's need. Surely it was seldom more true that " It is better to light a candle than to curse the dark ". Alongside that now familiar Chinese proverb we might well set this saying : " I am glad to think I am not bound to make the world go right, but only to discover and to do with cheerful heart the work that God appoints ". Here, in this great picture, is clearly and rewardingly set before us the work which God appoints in this world for which He cared and cares so deeply.

15

THE MINISTRY OF PRAYER—UNREALISED POSSIBILITIES

" Peter was kept in prison under constant watch, while the church kept praying fervently for him to God."—Acts xii. 5 (N.E.B.).

THERE is one aspect of service for others, and for the Kingdom of God, which it is dangerously easy to forget. Amid all the practical activities which can be so directly useful and so personally satisfying there is a real risk of our being so busy " getting things done " that we forget to pray. By that I do not mean simply that our positive activity will soon degenerate into a kind of hectic fussiness if we do not take time to lay hold on the resources of prayer. Even more important is our constant failure to include praying for other people as a part, and an absolutely indispensable part, of the service we can do for them. Praying for others, which is what we mean by " intercession ", is something we all become involved in, sooner or later. We may never feel the urge to pray for ourselves, but none of us can get very far through life without being driven to pray for others who are dear to us, because there is nothing else to do. When that time comes and we are driven to earnest and even desperate prayer for some loved one in direst need, everything depends on the way we then use prayer. It is bad for us, and it does not help our praying, if we are vague and uncertain. Recently I visited an old couple who were more or less " marooned " at the top of four flights of stairs, confined to that little world by increasing weakness and inability to face, except when one of them must, the long climb down to the shops for messages, and the much longer climb back up again. A kind and considerate friend had just given them a T.V. set, and had it installed and tested to make sure that it would function. They confessed that they were getting little good of it. She would not dare to touch it at all, and he was, frankly, frightened of it, not sure if he could adjust it properly, and therefore hardly using it. There they sat with a whole wealth and wonder of possibilities lying right to their hand, news and views, entertainment and instruction, even religious services such as those from which they were shut out now, to their great regret, all these were there for the taking. Yet they were getting practically no good out of it all. This is precisely our position with regard to this far greater marvel of intercessory prayer, simply because so many of us are so tentative and uncertain, not knowing where we are and, indeed, a little afraid of using this great gift. That is where this story from the Book of Acts can prove so suggestive and helpful. It calls us to " look in " at a group of people actually using this gift of prayer for others and making it work. The situation is clearly outlined and the story dramatically told. Peter has become the acknowledged leader of the young Christian Church, which is growing both in numbers and influence. Herod has beheaded James in a tentative bid for popularity with his Jewish subjects. Seeing that he has won their approval he has gone on to arrest Peter and is keeping him in custody until the Passover season has ended. Peter is under very close guard, which is not surprising because the authorities have had trouble with Peter breaking out before. Now it is the evening before the day when Herod plans to bring Peter out for public execution. While Peter is kept fast in prison the Church is praying for him. What can that situation say to us to-day about prayer for others ?

Prayer is an instrument of God's power whose range is unlimited, and which can reach to the heart of every situation. The prison in which Peter was kept was,

quite probably, the grim Fortress of Antonia, a great
citadel with thick walls and several successions of
gates. Right in the heart of the prison Peter was
kept by four soldiers, one chained to each ankle and
one to each wrist so that there was not the remotest
chance of Peter getting out. Yet the prayers of the
Church were getting in ; no walls, however high and
thick, and no gates of iron or doors of wood studded
with nails, no spears set across the doorways could
shut out prayer or prevent it from arriving at its
destination. That night a double vigil was being
maintained, and it is interesting to note that in our
text the word " kept " is used twice. It describes on
the one hand the vigil of the sentries and on the other
the vigil of the praying folk. There can be no doubt
that the former was powerless to render the latter
ineffective, for prayer can always reach to the heart of
every situation.

This is something we know instinctively, yet its
true wonder is hardly ever realised. Perhaps we can
do something to make it more real. You have a son,
a student, who is sitting his final examinations, which
are the culmination of years of study, and upon whose
outcome his whole future career will depend. You
cannot, for all your loving concern, go into the exam
room with him, or stand by his side at the orals, which
can be so " off-putting ", but your prayer can be with
him as a steadying influence and an " extra " beyond
all his toil and effort. Someone whom you love, and
with whose life, health and happiness your own life is
inextricably tied up, is going into the operating
theatre. The doors are clearly marked " No Admis-
sion " and you would not wish to enter there anyhow,
but your prayers, the expression and instrument of
your love, can pass through these doors without let or
hindrance. Even in the modern world, with the ends
of the earth brought together, you may often be painfully aware of the barrier of distance, with families
scattered over the face of the earth. Even with air

mail letters reducing the time of writing and receiving a reply to a matter of days, you can still feel cut-off. But none are ever out of the range of prayer and it still reaches out, in a wonderful fellowship to which miles do not matter and distance makes no difference at all.

It might seem that this line of thought must come to a dead end in the space age. Instead it has proved possible to give to it the most encouraging extension. When the American cosmonaut Colonel John Glenn was asked by a journalist if he had prayed (knowing he was a believing Christian) when he was in orbit, he replied quite simply and frankly : " No, I didn't pray because I hadn't time. There was too much to do. Anyhow I knew that the folks at home were seeing to the praying." So the range of prayer for others now extends into outer space, and where one unusually solitary human being is shut up in that fantastic " box of tricks " dealing with a highly complicated system of controls, another power, the power of prayer, is still at work. This truth holds good even where, humanly speaking, the destination of the prayer is not known. This was obviously the case with many of our war-time experiences. Some loved one had gone off with no address except an A.P.O. number, yet when we prayed we knew the prayer would reach its destination. It was true even when one such was posted " Missing ", for did they not write on the tomb of any Unknown Soldier " Known unto God " ? In the very different conditions of peace-time this still holds good. A mother whose son had simply disappeared seven years ago was lying gravely ill in hospital. " I have not the faintest idea where my son may be, in this country or overseas, but I still pray for him night and morning, for I remember that God knows where he is and He will hear my prayer." Imagine her joy when a few days later her Prodigal walked into the hospital. God does not operate any Dead Letter Service, no true prayer for others is ever returned " Not known ".

It is well to remember that distance and difficulties such as we have suggested above do not, in practice, constitute the most baffling problem. What about the situations where you are near, but still shut out ? There is the bitterness into which you are not permitted to penetrate. There is the problem which, for all your love, you are not allowed to share. You may be shut out, deliberately kept at arm's length, up against a blank wall, by son or daughter, husband or wife, but your prayer can still get in. Perhaps the most tragic barrier of all, the most impenetrable door, harder than the coldest steel, is that which exists where one person is ill with an incurable disease and the other, loving with an agony of compassion, cannot enter in to share the burden and the pain. There is a brave but tragic mutual conspiracy of silence. The mask must be donned every time you turn the handle of the bedroom door, the pretence must be kept up even if it breaks your heart. There remains one power which can overtop even this obstacle, which can pass through even this barrier. Nothing can shut out the power of prayer.

Prayer—sincere, believing prayer—makes a definite and positive contribution to every situation. The text states that : " the church kept praying fervently for him to God ". The exact wording is significant for it does not say merely that they kept praying. There is no particular value in going mechanically through some routine of praying for others. We need to guard carefully against the danger of degenerating into the techniques of prayer followed by the Tibetan who will write out a number of prayers, tie them to the spokes of an old bicycle wheel to which he has attached paddles, and then set it up in the bed of a burn. Every time the water turns the wheel that is a few more prayers said and virtue accrued. He will even tie a bunch of prayers to a dog's tail and with every wag of the tail more prayers are recorded ! Christian praying always involves what the Church was then doing for

Peter, entering imaginatively into his situation, trying
to share his thoughts as the hours slipped past and the
time of his expected execution drew near. Prayer, to
be effective, calls for a deliberate effort to realise the
situation, for only so can we pray fervently. This is
true, for example, of any prayer for those in need, for
the hungry or for refugees. We should do well to
pray for them with a picture on our mind's eye such
as we may have seen on *Panorama* ; we are more
likely to pray fervently if we think of one refugee
camp and one little group of starving children. Enter
in imaginatively into the situation of the person for
whom you are praying—that is priority No. 1. Then
we must also pray believingly. The people who were
praying in this case were first-century Christians ; the
thrill of their new-found faith was strong, they lived
on tip-toe of expectancy, they passionately believed in
the power of God. There was, admittedly, nothing
else they could do for Peter in that situation, but that
was not the spirit in which they were praying.

Do we not, all too often, pray believing deep down
that our praying cannot do any harm, but it is not
likely, in that particular situation, to do much good ?
The more impossible, humanly speaking, the situation
is, the more likely this is to be our attitude. To pray
like this is to defeat the whole object of prayer. But
what difference can praying make ? It makes a difference, at least, to know you are being prayed for ; and
most of us have known the wonderful experience, in
some dark hour of sorrow or of danger, of realising
that others are praying for us, and feeling their prayers,
like hands holding us up and steadying us. But
fervent, believing prayer does much more than that ;
it introduces a new and extra element into any situation. If we go back to our earlier picture of the
operating theatre, we can imagine the wonderful
team-work, and especially that of the theatre sister,
anticipating the surgeon's every movement, so that he
has only to hold out his hand and she puts the right

instrument into it. Prayer puts an extra instrument into the hand of God. Things happen to others when we pray for them which do not happen when we don't pray. It may be helpful to think of human hands which can be used as the instruments of some great purpose. There are the hands of the minister raised in Benediction over the people at the end of a service, reaching up and drawing down the power of God, and applying that power and grace to that particular set of people. There are the hands of a nurse, adjusting the bottle which gives the blood transfusion to the patient in whom the sands of life are running very low, so that this wonderful renewing agent is made available to this particular person. There are the hands of the technician switching on the power to a particular machine in a great factory, so that the driving energy with which the whole building is humming makes possible that particular piece of work. When we fold our hands in prayer for others we are never being idle, inactive, or merely submissive ; we are making precisely that quality of real difference, that kind of positive contribution to the situation. In this busy, hurried world, when we are so anxiously concerned to get things done, and produce results, in the home, in the church, in the community, we should do well to stop and listen to this challenge to pray, not to neglect the unlimited potential of the definite and positive contribution which fervent and believing prayer can still make to any situation. Prayer was made " for him . . . to God ".

Prayer, real, fervent, believing prayer, unlocks possibilities beyond our power to imagine. Does praying produce results in this case of Peter and the Church ? All through the story there are two pictures which are kept side by side. Indeed, it is as if, in terms of TV, the producer kept switching us, the viewers, from one camera to the other. We see, on the one hand, the Church praying, the little group of Christian folk, apparently so pathetically helpless, considering the strength of the prison and the care taken to guard Peter. Then we see Peter asleep, chained between the sentries. The fact that he is sleeping soundly and peacefully under such conditions may be a tribute already to the power of their praying. Then comes the dramatic rescue. The more often I read the story, especially in the New English Bible version, the more I feel convinced that the " angel " was a human messenger, an instrument of God's purpose. Read the details, the very graphic, human details of the story, and it savours exactly of a *Scarlet Pimpernel* type of rescue. To begin with, Peter doesn't believe that it is happening ; he is out on the street before it dawns upon him that this is not a vision, a piece of wishful thinking on his part. He goes straight to the house of Mary, the mother of John Mark, where they are praying for him. He knocks, and has difficulty in getting an answer, for the people inside the house are too busy praying for him to hear him knock. The servant lass, Rhoda, goes to the door, hears his voice, and is so excited that, instead of opening the door she hurries back in to break up the prayer-meeting with her news. They cannot believe it ; the precise thing they have been praying for has happened, and they just don't believe it. They think of every other explanation except the wonderful truth, that their prayers, offered continuously, fervently, and believingly, have been gloriously answered.

Surely this old story, told so clearly and directly that it still comes alive readily to our minds and hearts, is reminding us very forcibly that prayer for others unlocks unlimited possibilities beyond our imagining. These possibilities may be realised through God's use of human agents. If the " angel " in the story of Peter was a human being who succeeded in drugging the sentries, and getting the keys, both of the doors and of the fetters that held Peter ; if the famous iron gate leading to the city (about which

many a forceful sermon has been preached !) opened
of its own accord because an accomplice was waiting
to open it, is this any less a miracle of God's deliver-
ance ? God very often uses human agents for the
answering of our prayers for others. This is obviously
true in the case, for instance, of a surgeon, who can
tease a tumour from the brain and give back not only
life but sanity and normality to someone very dear.
It is true on the more ordinary human level of the
constant intermeshing of life with life. We who live
in the space age should find it less difficult than ever
to imagine how God could be able to do this. The
world in which human skill and knowledge can produce
a capsule which will carry a human being into orbit,
high above the earth ; in which conditions are created
for maintaining life as we know it ; a capsule which is
kept under control, both at so remote a distance,
and locally by the man inside ; from which messages
and data are sent out continually, so that communication is continually maintained ; a capsule whose
incredible speed can be slowed down for safe re-entry
into the atmosphere and brought back to within a few
miles of the nearest waiting ship—a world which now
takes this for granted should not find it difficult that
God should so control and direct human life that He
can and does answer prayer.

Every minister could quote many examples of
things happening to real people within his own experience which he can only explain by saying that they
were an answer to prayer. There has never been any
great movement of discovery or renewal within the
history of the Christian Church which was not connected with a group or groups of people praying. On
the level of personal, human relationships and of
direct and clamant human need, even in " the affluent
society " the demand for the kind of results which
accrue only from prayer grows greater rather than
less. There no evidence that, as was said thirty
years ago by a believer in the self-sufficiency of man :

" God becomes increasingly unnecessary ". There is also ample evidence that the Church everywhere throughout the world is crying out for that spiritual renewal which can only come when throughout the Church groups of believing people keep praying fervently.

16

YOUR GOD IS TOO SMALL

" The Lord is God of the hills, but he is not God of the valleys."
—1 Kings xx. 28.

THOSE of us who count ourselves " inside " the
Church, or as the Psalm expresses it, " Even
those that be of Israel's race, near to His grace ",
must always hold, at least in the background of our
thinking, those who are " outside ", or on the fringes
of the Church. We cannot help being aware that they
are very many, and very frequently they compel our
attention. We have no right ever to think of them
patronisingly, but surely, rather, with a sense of
responsibility and self-criticism, remembering that
their numbers are the measure of our failure, in a
land where the Christian faith has been at work for so
many centuries. Suppose we start to think of their
position, and so work inwards to ourselves and our
own situation. There is first the attitude of the out-
and-out atheist whose unbelief is a matter of policy,
part of a political ideology, as in world-wide Communism. At the same time, it is well to realise that in
the countries of the West there are not so very many
who hold atheism as an article of belief. No, that is
not our danger. Our trouble is that for every one
who is a convinced atheist, there are a hundred who
are " practising " atheists, that is, they live from day
to day as if God were not ; they may on special
occasions go through the outward motions of religion
but for the most part God is not in all their thoughts.
Then there is the attitude of agnosticism which
maintains that there may be a God or there may not,
but in either case we cannot know ; and those who
hold this faith are often truly reverent, earnest, and

sincere. Admittedly agnosticism can sometimes be an excuse for refusing to take the trouble of making up one's own mind about religious reality, or even at times a refuge from moral issues, but it can be a quite honest belief.

By far the most common of all forms of " unbelief ", however, that which is in many ways most dangerous and harmful, is to hold a too-limited idea of God, like the Syrians in the background of our text. This attitude affects us all, somewhere, sometime ; it even affects some of us all the time. This is the tragedy of real unbelief, which lowers the tone and temperature of spiritual life all over the English-speaking world— " Your God is too small, He is not great enough ". Let us look at some of the limited ideas men have held and now hold, and see how in Christ we are delivered into greater ideas of God. Learning to know God can be, after all, like going up the Empire State Building in New York ; you can walk up one flight of stairs and look out from a first-floor window, and be content with the limited view you will get there. Most people who go there at all prefer to take the high-speed elevators right to the top and command the whole tremendous panorama.

Our first limited idea is that God is here but not there, in one place but not in another. This was the view held by the Syrians, that the God of the Israelites was effective, He functioned and was so powerful that you could not beat Him, or His people in the hills. If you could induce the Israelites to fight in the valleys their God would not be able to give them victory, for He was only effective on His own ground. We find this idea, that God is in one place but not in another, gradually being outgrown throughout the Old Testament. Jacob lies down to an uneasy rest on the stony slopes of Bethel and discovers, to his complete surprise : " Surely the Lord is in this place, and I knew it not ". The writer of the glorious Psalm cxxxix. builds up his sense of the presence of God everywhere, and cries with wonder : " Even there shall thy hand lead me . . . the darkness and the light are both alike to thee ". In the Book of Jonah the prophet, having refused to do what God commanded, books a passage on a ship bound for the furthest end of the Mediterranean, the idea being that every league he sails westward he will be getting further and further from the authority of God whose writ runs only in Palestine. The whole controversial business of the great fish simply proves to Jonah how wrong he was. The bitter experience of exile carried this discovery a great stage further, for the Jews in Babylon might still believe that God was specially present in Jerusalem, yet He was not removed from them when they were compelled to sing the Lord's song in a strange land.

Then came Jesus, refuting for ever the idea that God can be up there in the glittering immensity of the starry heavens, but not down here in the frailty of a tiny child ; that God is to be found among the lamps and sacred vessels in a temple, but not in the straw and the feeding trough of a stable. He entered into everything, revealing the presence of God in the whole fabric of our ordinary human experience. At the end His story declared this quite awe-ful thing, it dared to say, what is entirely shocking, that God could be present on a Cross of shame, and tragedy, and utter defeat. When, at the moment when Jesus died, the veil of the Temple was rent in twain that was the end of the idea that God is confined to any one type of place. There is a great and salutary lesson here that we all need constantly to re-learn. We, too, have special sacred places, such as the church in which we normally worship ; that special building by its unusual and " separate " character is of immense benefit in helping us to realise the presence of God. We expect God to be there, especially if our church is an old foundation, on a spot to which many generations have come before us ; there we submit, naturally, to His judgment, there we reach out expectantly for His strength. Then we go away from the specially sacred place, and we act as if we left God behind, as if He were only there, and not here in the everyday world which, after all, occupies so large a proportion of our time and interest.

We are all affected by this attitude, we all do it. We have two standards between which we continually " commute ". When we are in church we sincerely desire to learn what God wants and to do it, for this is the way to see that His will is done, in earth as it is in heaven. When we leave the church behind we want to do what everybody else does, we accept and conform to the standards of the world, and this may involve a very real change. When we are in church we are gratefully conscious of great resources ; amid the strains and stresses of everyday living we behave, we become overstrained, we fail, as if we had no resources other than our own. When we sit in church with our hands folded, or bow in prayer we have one kind of concern, which brings back poise and serenity to life because it is God-centred ; amid the hectic activity which we follow from day to day we have a totally different set of concerns bringing only hurry and heat because they tend to be self-centred instead. This is all wrong, even if it is perfectly natural and understandable. We ministers do it too, though with least excuse. After all, we pray not only in church, in leading public worship ; we pray over a child, God's newest gift to a home; we pray by many a bedside in hospital; we pray, all too often, in a darkened home. We do that on the assumption that God is everywhere present and everywhere to be found. Jesus, after all, did not say " I am with you one day a week in church " ; what He did say was " I am with you all the days ".

It is because we think this way that we believe, too often, that God can be called in and then discharged when He has served our turn. To say this sounds positively blasphemous and irreverent, but it is true and it is very common and very subtle. Again, this attitude runs all through the Old Testament. Continually we read, generation after generation, that the people cried to God in their need and He delivered them. When the danger passed they forgot God and went their own way again. This still goes on, and well do we know it. We are, let us not forget it, the nation who crowded the churches at the time of Dunkirk in May 1940 and again at the time of D-Day in June 1944, and look at us now ! We all do this, it is a perfectly normal human failing ; when the sun is shining God fades into the background of life, but we run instinctively to Him when fear lays its cold hand on our hearts, or we face some hopeless situation we simply cannot handle. As an old Negro Christian once said : " When I want to do dis thing, I puts de Lord up on de shelf. When it is over and done with I takes Him down again." He was only being honest about something we all do continually.

Along with this attitude goes the idea of a God whose services can somehow be bought, paid for in some kind of currency, and then claimed as a right thereafter. This is one rather subtle danger of our recent emphasis on Christian Stewardship. When stewardship is limited to money, as it is in so many situations where a commercial firm is called in to organize increased Christian liberality, this " heresy " lies at the door, especially in a civilisation which is already too much materially-minded. We may give the impression that once I have paid a little more money to the church I have discharged my total obligation to Jesus Christ, and, by a quite logical process of thought that I have paid a retaining fee on the services of Almighty God. What appals me, personally, and every other minister, surely, when he sees it, is the attitude of so many church members to whom this is all that their church membership seems to mean. By the vows they have taken, by their very occasional attendance at church, by their usually disgracefully meagre and casual giving of their money, in a purely token fashion, they have paid their annual premium to yet another beneficial " club " and they are bound to be " in benefit " ! Every minister knows that this is no caricature but is a grim reality.

For all of us it is a question of the way we look at our relationships with God, basically, the way we think of Him. If my giving is an expression of my desire to serve Him, if in seeking to exercise steward-ship of my time and talents I am putting myself at His disposal, and not, in some subtle way, making sure He will be at my disposal when I want Him, then all is well. This is the fundamental unbelief which undermines religion completely, and vitiates any good I may do through my service for God in His Church ; it is the belief that God is there to serve me, to help me through, to see that I am all right. Perhaps an extreme instance will illustrate what we mean. A woman in a Scottish housing scheme had become an " addict " of the Bingo craze. One evening she had arranged for a fifteen-year-old girl to come and " baby-sit ", but the girl had not arrived by the time the mother had to go out for her evening's entertainment. She took a chance and left her three children, aged seven, five, and three in the house alone. The three-year-old, ready for bed, stumbled against the electric radiator and went up in flames. The seven-year-old did the best she could think of and flung a pail of water over the screaming child. The child simply died. When the minister went to see the mother about the funeral she was quite mystified by the whole situation, regarding it as a grave failure of God's providence rather than a tragic breakdown of her own motherly care. " God must be queer ", she said. " Does He not want us to enjoy ourselves ? " Surely this is a glaring instance where " Your God is too small ", a God who could be expected to " drop in " magically to save such a situation and then retire humbly to the background once again.

There is, finally, the idea that God can be defeated,

that some power may prove stronger, greater, more effective than God. This was the attitude of the Syrians, that if they could find the right place to fight, then they could beat God. Here is the source of many of our own doubts and difficulties. Mere human cleverness, culminating in the era of space-flight, has made the gospel apparently more difficult to accept. God becomes ever-increasingly unnecessary. Our new-found self-sufficiency, our reaching up and faring forth into outer space seem to have made irrelevant the coming down and coming in of God from above and from the outside. We may still sing—

" Lord of all being, throned afar,
     Thy glory flames from sun and star ;
     Centre and soul of every sphere,
     Yet to each loving heart how near ! "

but what does this mean, any more, now that we our-selves have started hobnobbing with the stars them-selves ? It is high time we set about " dreaming a greater God ". When we see on television a May Day parade of armed might in Red Square in Moscow, the marching men who are only a few of the ranks of the marching millions ; when we see the sinister rockets towed through the Square on their huge carriers, it is quite natural to assume that Communism, which is so strong, so ruthless, and so efficient, might even defeat God and destroy His purpose. The trouble is that our God is too small, He no longer bulks large enough in our own thinking to be great enough to save His world. When we look forward at all we picture, in our blacker moods, the world burning itself out in some cataclysm of criminal folly, started, it may be, by some nation or leader who did not really mean this to happen, and that is the end of this great costly human experiment into which God has put so much of Himself.

The same is true at a much more personal and intimate level, when we find ourselves having to deal with the abiding realities, the ancient enemies of sin and failure, suffering and death. In spite of the affluent society, and notwithstanding all the beneficent operations of the Welfare State, nothing can completely " cushion " and insulate us against these grim realities ; sooner or later we all experience them. These ancient enemies defeat our purposes, and defy our love. You go into a hospital ward and see a small child, terribly burned, or smashed up in an accident. You know that human skill will patch him up wonderfully and give him some sort of a life, but it can never be free from handicap—the normal, carefree kind of life to which any child is entitled. It is almost inevitable to assume that in that life and in that degree the purpose of God's love is defeated. Or you have to visit a woman suffering from cancer in the neck and throat. Any conversation is hopelessly one-sided, for her vocal chords are gone, and her side of the conversation must be carried out by writing painfully on a paper pad. You know perfectly well, from long experience, that in spite of all pain-killing drugs, that woman will slowly disintegrate, until she is, in all probability a travesty of the lovely, laughing, vital person you have known. You realise that when death comes it will come not, in a case like this, as the last enemy, but as the servant of God's purpose, bringing release, if not to a larger life, then at least into a blessed nothingness, where pain shall be no more. Yet, realising this, one is left with the inescapable impression that here, too, the purpose of God's love must have been defeated. The only answer to this human situation, or to the larger, world-wide situation of threat and fear is to get back to the Cross of Christ, and see there amid the tragedy, the suffering, and the utter defeat, a God so great that He cannot in the end be defeated. The darkness and the light are both alike to His love and saving power, and though any of us be called upon to make our bed in hell, even there His hand shall lead us. Anything less than this, and your God is too small.

17

THE VISION THAT MUST BE OBEYED

"I was not disobedient unto the heavenly vision."—Acts
xxvi. 19.

THESE are the words of a man looking back on the
greatest experience of his life, standing, as it
were, on the water-shed of all that has happened to
him. He is looking back on the great day when the
unseen world broke in and the Risen Christ became
inescapably real to him, so real that in making a list
of the Resurrection appearances of our Lord he includes
this experience of his as being in precisely the same
category. He is describing it thirty years after it
happened, yet it is as vivid as if it had happened only
that morning. Because of Paul's experience on the
Damascus road life was never the same again.

If one were to ask the average congregation how
many have had any such experience the great majority
would protest : " It has never been like that with me ;
I have never had anything faintly approaching that
kind of experience ". Yet I am sure that, if we look
under the surface, the essence of Paul's vital experience
is not nearly so rare as we think. Look back and ask
yourself if there has never been a time when for you
the two worlds came very close, the seen and the
unseen, the temporal and the eternal, so close that the
veil of sense grew very thin indeed. One of the more
effective tricks of TV production is made possible by
the use of two cameras, and the fading in and out of
two pictures, imposed one upon the other. You are
seeing and hearing, perhaps, the B.B.C. Orchestra
playing Mendelssohn's familiar *Fingal's Cave Overture*,
and to begin with you see only the orchestra. Then
you become aware that through the movement of the

violin bows and the conductor's baton you are sensing the shape of a great cliff, and through the orchestra there are washing back and forward great waves. Gradually the orchestra fades out altogether and you are seeing the waves of the Atlantic surging in and out of Fingal's Cave. Has some such merging of the two worlds never happened to you ? Perhaps it was at a moment of great joy when out of your wonder of happiness God became wonderfully real. Perhaps it was in an hour of great danger when you felt beneath you, strong and sustaining and wonderfully real, the everlasting arms. Perhaps it was in some bitter hour of great sorrow, when the waves and billows went over you, yet you rose again.

Perhaps you still insist : " No. Nothing faintly like that has ever happened to me." Then, have you even had the experience of going, say, to an Easter Communion ? The beauty of the flowers, the loveliness of the day, some word sung or spoken, or just the meaning and message of the sacrament spoke home to your heart and soul. This can and does happen to any of us. If it does happen, happen how it may, then after the experience is gone from us it leaves a challenge. When the thrill and expectancy are over, when the flowers and the glory alike have faded, when the ordinariness of life gets us down, what do we do then ? What do we do with the moments of vision, which somehow, sometime, in some degree, God grants to each of us ?

Do we live up to the moment of vision, or down to the ordinariness of life ? Paul must often have had good cause to doubt the reality of his own great experience. At this point in the Book of Acts he is about to enter on the final stage of his career and already he has much bitter experience behind him. In 2 Corinthians he details his own record of effort and suffering, and it is a record of quite incredible endurance, an amazing achievement for a man who was never, as we should say, one hundred per cent fit.

He must many times have known no reality but pain, his back bruised and broken from a Jewish beating. When he was stoned and left for dead and came back out of the mists of unconsciousness it was not easy to keep his vision. When he was adrift in the open sea, one tiny speck of humanity in the waste of waters, he must have wondered about the purpose. Many, many voices from around him and within must have said to him : " Where is your vision now ? " Resolutely he reminded himself that the unseen Presence was real everywhere, as real in a water-logged derelict drifting towards the rocks of Malta as on the Damascus road. Constantly he insisted that there was a Joy which sought him even through pain. He refused with wonderful resolution ever to let his vision go and be dragged down to the ordinariness of life.

Do not let go your vision. There are more than plenty influences which combine and conspire to drag down our spirits. From stage and screen, both in the cinema and on television, from the printed page and by the spoken word, they take all that is dull and drab, sordid, suggestive or positively degrading, and they cry to us : " This is life. This alone is real." But so are our moments of vision and we must not allow them ever to become unreal. These moments of vision, of uplifting dreams and high ideals come to us and we tend to get over them. In Myrtle Reed's novel *Spinner in the Sun* an old doctor is talking to his young son who has just qualified and is all starry-eyed about the high ideals of his noble profession. The older man is not just being cynical, he is wanting to prevent his son from being too easily hurt. He says : " You'll get over it. When you've been called out in the middle of the night to a sick child who has been ill since the morning, but the mother couldn't be bothered to send for you sooner ; when you've delivered a healthy child to a couple who won't even give you thanks— you'll get over it." This is true and understandable, but we must resist the tendency to " get over it ". If

you have prepared carefully for several weeks for the
outward act of " joining the Church ", come to church
and taken your vows on Good Friday, and then come
to your first Communion in the glory of an Easter Day,
there is something wrong with you if you are not in
the least " starry-eyed " about the experience. But
the next week you come down to earth with a bump ;
you come up against one of those professing Christians
whose conduct in terms of personal relationships is a
flagrant denial of the faith they profess, or you let
yourself down. Resist like the plague the strong
temptation to " get over it ".

Again and again in life one finds that nothing is so
important as to recapture one's vision. One Scots
minister of a large congregation holds annually a
Service of Rededication for all the couples he has
married in the past year. What is that likely to do
for them ? Remind them of the vows they took ?
Yes, and that can prove most salutary. But it is
much more important to give them back the vision,
the dreams, the hopes and ideals they had in the
beginning. One day in 1940, when working on welfare
at Kyle of Lochalsh, I went with my family on a quick
tour of the Isle of Skye. We came down to the south-
west corner at the village of Elgol and looked straight
across to the fantastic range of the Cuillins. In the
foreground was the great sweep of the sea, the waves
dancing in the sunshine ; then came the mountains
rising in a solid mass to their jagged summits, cut out
as it were with a fretsaw, and the most wonderful
plum coloured shade. I know that others have gone
to the same spot and seen that same vista rain-
drenched, overcast by brooding clouds and felt it to
be sinister and threatening. I can only remember
the Cuillins as I saw them that day, in that moment of
unrivalled vision. The familiar story is told of two
eminent Scots divines walking in the Border hills and
seeing a kite flying from beyond the far slope of the
next rise, flying " brawly " in a good breeze. As they

drew near they realised that it was being flown, and flown skilfully, by a small boy, drawing in the string at the right moment, and letting it go when he should. On his face was the wrapt expression of a boy whose kite is flying well, but his eyes were blind. One of the men said to him : " Do you not miss a lot flying your kite, when you cannot see it ? " " Maybe I can't see it," replied the boy, " but I can feel it tug." Get back your vision. Even if you cannot see it clearly any more you can at least feel it tug.

Do I set about bringing the vision into touch with real life ? Paul quite deliberately and continually did this. There is a kind of angle-poise lamp, set on a firm base and hinged at every joint in such a way that it is capable of being moved in any direction, so that you can focus it precisely on any particular situation. You can bring its light down and concentrate it on that intricate piece of embroidery or that complicated formula whose figures are difficult to read. This is precisely what Paul did with the light of his great vision ; he brought it down and focused it on every situation. The bitter opposition of the Jews, their plots against his life, the long delay before he was brought to trial, all these were set in the light of the purpose he saw on the Damascus road. In the shipwreck he proved to be the only calm man in the lot ; on the tossing, wave-swept deck he took bread and made it a Sacrament, because he saw even that situation in the light of his vision. That is what our moments of vision are granted for. This theme runs through and through the New Testament. Some hardy, down-to-earth shepherds are granted a vision on the hills above Bethlehem ; they stumble, starry-eyed, through the dark streets, and find a Baby, born in a stable and lying in a manger, but they see the meaning behind the ordinariness because for this they were granted the vision. Jesus comes up out of the water of Jordan at His Baptism ; He sees the Spirit descending upon Him like a dove ; then He goes straight into the desert to face the temptations, for which the vision will strengthen Him. He prays in the Garden of Gethsemane in a thrice-repeated agony of decision ; an angel appears to strengthen Him, and the next moment Judas and the guards arrive to arrest Him.

How do we use our moments of vision ? Do we treat them like a sprig of faded white heather from a wedding bouquet, to be carefully preserved between the pages of a Bible that is none too often used ? Is our moment of vision regarded as something to be sheltered and isolated, or is it meant to be deliberately related to life ? That popular TV programme, *This Is Your Life*, once told the story of a District Nurse in a scattered rural area of Scotland. It described how she went, on a wild night, to deliver a baby in a tinker's encampment. The mother apologised for the poor kind of home in which the nurse would have to do her work. The nurse replied quite simply : " The greatest Baby ever born was born in a far worse place than this ". Talk about bringing the light down and focusing it on real situations ! A little girl of three-and-a-bit was taken to church last Christmas for the first time. She started singing " Away in a Manger " and they couldn't get her to stop. She was taken for the second time on Easter Sunday. There was a lot of singing in one of the hymns of a word " Alleluia ! " She didn't understand all of the hymn, but whenever it came to " Alleluia " she joined in. She did realise that everyone was being happy, because Jesus was alive, and that this created a new happiness, touching everything in life. The next day she came out into the garden, looked round on that lovely morning, and cried out ! " Daddy's got a bong-fire. Alleluia ! " She had got the idea all right, an idea we all need in these days of so much doubt, depression, and defeatism to rediscover. I do not have to face this problem alone—Alleluia. I do not require to sort out this tangled situation in my own strength—Alleluia. I need not try to make this awkward choice in my own wisdom alone—Alleluia. Bring the vision down to earth.

Do I keep my moment of vision to myself or do I share it with others ? Paul was constantly talking of his great moment, this break-in, this take-over that had changed his whole life. He did that for two reasons. First, this was far too big to keep to himself ; he spoke about it to others because he simply could not help it. How big in my life is any moment of vision that has been granted to me ? Do I say of it, in effect : " This is real, this is wonderful, but I can keep it all to myself. This is private and personal and intimate ; it is a secret matter between me and God " ? Can you imagine a chronic sufferer from arthritis, never out of pain day or night, constantly and increasingly handicapped, whose doctor has tried on her a new drug that has given complete relief from pain and considerable recovery of movement ? She has a friend and fellow-sufferer, with whom for years she has compared notes, both about symptoms and treatments. Could she possibly keep this to herself and say nothing about it to another in the same desperate need ? Surely if I have had any kind of vision of the reality which is in Christ, it is much too big to keep to myself.

The other reason why Paul was always talking of his experience was that he had quite deliberately decided it would help others. This is more than ever true to-day. All around us, day and daily, there are people like ourselves, desperately needing and increasingly longing for a faith that is real, and vital and relevant ; a faith that reaches out and touches real situations. There is a growing sense of the emptiness of life, however prosperous and secure, without a true and living faith which will relate directly to the facts of the life that real people live. Very many ordinary people write off a large percentage of what we ministers say, simply because it is our job to say this kind of thing. But let one ordinary woman on *Woman's Hour* on the radio describe how she found a faith which enabled her to handle the heartbreak of a broken marriage, or to deal with the problem of teaching her own children, and thousands of other women will " lap it up ", for that is precisely what they are looking for. If we have really found the secret of victorious and radiant living let us make a point of sharing it with others.

I have in my study a life-size copy of the painting of the head of Christ by Herbert Beecroft, entitled *The Lord Turned and Looked on Peter*. Some sixteen years ago a lady in my congregation, as a member of the Tea Committee at a Garden Fete, passing in and out through the study, saw that picture, perhaps four times. A few months later she was critically ill in a Nursing Home, suffering from cancer from which eventually she died. One day, when I went to see her, I found her looking exhausted but astonishingly peaceful. After a little she said to me : " A wonderful thing happened to me last night. They had given me the usual jag to deaden the pain and give me some sleep. About two in the morning the effect had already worn off and I was in the most incredible agony, so that I felt I just couldn't stand any more. Then, suddenly, on that blank wall in this room I seemed to see the picture of Christ which you have in your study. There was a wonderful light on the picture—not a light shining on the picture, but, as it were, a light shining out from the picture. The Face smiled on me in such infinite love and compassion that I felt I could stand anything." From that moment I felt that it was not pain, disease and death that was winning the victory, it was her faith. Now, this was a very private and personal experience ; she could easily have kept it to herself, but she chose to tell me. Sixteen years later I was in the same room. The entire Nursing Home had been altered and renovated out of recognition and the room itself was completely redecorated, but to me it was still the room where that experience had been known and passed on. The patient this time was a woman, thoughtful, intelligent and sensitive, who had known ten years of pain and weakness. I told her the other woman's story and she was greatly moved and inspired by it. She went home, apparently very much improved, and then died, quite suddenly and without any warning. I like to think that she faced the last Enemy, with a clear picture shining before her of the love and compassion of the Lord of Life, who is the Conqueror of death, because another woman was given a moment of vision, and chose not to keep it to herself but to share it with others.